Ple

Y

egan in**15**

Vegan in 15

Delicious plant-based recipes
you can cook in 15 mins or less

KATE FORD

Published in 2017 by
Short Books, Unit 316, ScreenWorks, 22 Highbury Grove,
London, N5 2ER

10 9 8 7 6 5 4 3 2 1

A CIP catalogue record for this book
is available from the British Library.

ISBN: 978-1-78072-300-6

Photographs © Romas Foord
Cover design by Georgia Vaux
Cover photo © Romas Foord
Printed at CPI Group (UK) Ltd, Croydon, CR0 4YY

15-Minute Recipes

1. Easy Brunch

Griddled Asparagus with Lemony Sauce on Crumpets
Blackberry Ripple Yoghurt Pots with Almond Crunch
Smoky 'Full English' on Toast
Banana & Pecan Pancakes with Maple Syrup
Smashed Avocado on Toast with Crispy Spring
  Onions and Chilli Yoghurt
Creamy Peach Breakfast Smoothie
Bubble and Squeak Fry-Up with Grilled Tomatoes
Hazelnut and Plum Porridge with Pumpkin Seeds

2. Speedy Soups

Chunky Green Minestrone with Curly Kale
Thai Sweet Potato and Coconut Soup
Oyster Mushroom Tom Yum Soup with Rice Noodles
Creamy Sweetcorn and Chilli Chowder with Garlic
  Bread
Gently Curried Lentil Soup
Tuscan Borlotti Bean Soup with Orzo
Mixed Mushroom Curry Laksa

3. Salads

Spring Greens Giant Couscous with Avocado
Grilled Portobello and Cherry Tomato Panzanella
Warm Puy Lentil and Beetroot Salad
Bright Green Freekeh Salad
Crunchy Thai Vegetable and Peanut Salad
Beetroot and Apple Salad with Walnuts and Yoghurt
Tenderstem, Cucumber and Soba Noodle Salad
Speedy Spinach Falafels with Carrot and Apple Salad

4. Fast Lunch

Pitta Stuffed with Harissa Chickpeas and Hummus
Posh Noodle Pot with Chilli Peanuts
Broccoli and Kale Pine Nut Pizza
Artichoke and Watercress Brown Rice with Pine Nuts
Speedy Bean Burger with Gherkins and Mustard Mayo
Sherry and Thyme Garlicky Mushrooms on Toast
Preserved Lemon and Apricot Couscous with Za'tar
  Almonds
Black Bean Tacos with Avocado and Roasted Peppers

5. Small Plates

Cannellini Beans and Cavolo Nero
Peanut Vietnamese Rolls
Curried Lentils with Spiced Cauliflower
Pea Pâté with Pea Shoots on Sourdough Toast
Courgetti and Sweetcorn Fritters with Coconut
  Yoghurt
Smoky 'Cowboy Beans'
Broad Beans and Asparagus with Lemon Breadcrumbs
French Beans and New Potatoes with Basil Pesto

6. Main Dishes

One-Pot Linguine with Olives, Capers and Sun-Dried
  Tomatoes
Speedy Cauliflower and Chard Spelt Risotto
Creamy Chickpea and Kale Curry with Poppadoms
Savoy and Sesame Flat Noodles with Marinated Tofu
Spelt Spaghetti with Walnuts and Purple Sprouting
  Broccoli
Stir-Fried Tenderstem and Kale with Pesto Butter Bean
  Mash
Tahini and Cashew Quinoa Bowl with Garlic and
  Ginger Mushrooms
Creamy Fusilli with Mushrooms and White Wine
Green Pea and New Potato Nutty Biryani
Portobello Mushroom Stroganoff

Chapatti Wraps with Spiced Chickpeas, Baby
  Spinach and Coconut Yoghurt
Broad Bean, Fennel and Baby Carrot Pilaff
Peanut and Ginger Soba Noodles with Chestnut
  Mushrooms
Sticky Black Bean Tofu with Cashew Fried Rice
Five-Spice Shiitake with Chinese Vegetables
Quick Ratatouille with Lemony Chickpea Mash

7. Decadent Desserts

Lemon and Poppy Seed Waffles with Elderflower
  Summer Fruits
Gooey Chocolate and Pear Pudding
Banoffee 'Cheese-cake' Pots
Amaretto-Sozzled Figs with Candied Walnut Crunch
Caramelised Peaches on French Toast
Quick Raspberry Trifles
Chocolate and Peanut Butter 'Freakshake'
Oreo Knickerbocker Glory
Chocolate, Chilli and Pistachio Dipped Strawberries
Quick Rhubarb and Crumble Custard Pots
Chocolate and Hazelnut Grilled Banana Splits
Salted Caramel Chocolate Mousse Cups

Introduction

There seems to be something of a revolution happening out there. With each year that passes, veganism becomes more mainstream. Vegans are no longer just ageing hippies sitting in garishly decorated cafés nibbling mung beans. Being an animal rights activist or an eco-warrior is no longer a pre-requisite for a plant-based diet. These days it is enough to have the desire to shop and eat in a way that treads as lightly as possible on our fragile planet and which doesn't involve the suffering of animals, while lightening the load on our bodies too. What's not to like?

Well, quite a lot apparently. There are so many misconceptions about vegan food: that it tastes bland or even 'weird'; that it is somehow difficult or time-consuming to prepare; that you need all sorts of strange ingredients which you won't find in your local supermarket, and that if you really enjoy cooking (and eating), it will be a great sacrifice.

None of these are remotely true – which is why I wanted to write this book. I'm not here to tell you why you should eat less meat and dairy, nor why you should go vegan. Instead, if you are thinking about it, or have decided to do so, I hope simply to show you that you can eat incredibly tasty food which doesn't take hours to prepare or involve trips to multiple health food shops for obscure ingredients.

These recipes aren't gluten-free, sugar-free, low-calorie, low-carb, paleo or detoxing. They won't necessarily give you an 'inner glow', a 'bikini-ready beach-body', or cure medical ailments. They just offer really good food which is quick and easy to make, and which happens to be vegan. I'm passionate about writing recipes which look and taste like the sort of food you see in mainstream cookery books and magazines – recipes, above all, which will lift your spirits when you've had 'that' conversation about protein with a well-meaning friend for the hundredth time.

Three years ago, having been vegetarian since the age of seven, I signed up for 'Veganuary'.

Veganuary, for those of you who haven't yet heard of it, is a global charitable initiative which encourages people to go vegan for the month of January – and provides all the information they might need to persuade them to convert to a plant-based diet.

I was fairly confident that going vegan would not prove to be an insurmountable challenge, but it turned out to be quite a learning curve. I struggled at first to come up with ideas for what on earth to eat; I struggled with reading labels, finding vegan snacks and lunches on the go and particularly with eating out. But as the days went on, it got easier, and at the end of the month I felt not just cleaner and lighter, but filled with a nagging feeling that this was somehow the 'right' way to eat.

A year later, I signed up to Veganuary once again, and this time planned my meals in advance, shopped wisely, kept lists of which brands I could and couldn't buy and found some really good substitutions to vegan-ise many of my favourite weeknight suppers. This time, my vegan month was much more enjoyable. I ate far tastier food and missed dairy products less than I had done at my first attempt.

By the time I signed up for my third Veganuary in January 2016, I had been actively trying to cut out the 'hidden' eggs and dairy lurking in my weekly grocery shop for a while. My vegetarian food blog, The Veg Space, turned vegan for the month too, and I decided to post pictures of my dinner on instagram every night to show my followers what vegans really eat.

When the month was over, vegan habits had

'stuck', and I took the decision that my blog would stay vegan and my own everyday diet would remain mainly plant-based. I am not perfect, and while I can't claim to be among Britain's half a million fully-fledged vegans, the recipes in this book are 100% vegan and reflect the way I eat at home almost every day.

Three years of experimenting with veganism have made me realise that usually the smallest of tweaks and substitutions to your favourite recipes can make them fully plant-based, while still tasting great. And these tricks are usually no more hassle than reaching for a different shelf at your local supermarket, or reading the label on a couple of packets before you find the one that is egg-free. Yes, shopping and cooking vegan takes a bit of getting used to, but I hope that by taking 15 minutes of your time to try one of these recipes each evening, you will quickly realise how easy and delicious veganism can be.

Whether you've bought this book because you are thinking of going vegan, or just want to reduce the amount of meat and dairy in your diet, welcome! My hope is that as you start to enjoy the myriad flavours from around the world that can make up a varied, healthy, animal-free diet, you might just choose to do it a bit more often, if not every day.

Kate Ford, Nov 2016

Going Vegan: Top Tips

1. Just do it! Going vegan isn't nearly as difficult as you might imagine. This is a great time to be trying it – I can hardly keep up with the growing list of dairy-free products in supermarkets, and as the competition in the sector is increasing, so too is the quality and flavour of the new products on the shelves. There are also many more options for eating out than there were just a few years ago, and a multitude of recipes on the internet and new cookbooks mean that cooking delicious and varied vegan food at home has never been easier.

2. Take part in a 30-day vegan challenge. A one-month challenge is a great way to really change habits and get to grips with a new way of eating. I took part in 'Veganuary' (a vegan January) for three years running, which was a great experience. By immersing yourself in a vegan diet for a whole month rather

than, say, once a week, you learn by necessity how to eat and snack from a vegan fridge, how to throw together last-minute vegan suppers on the run, how to shop differently, read labels more carefully, and which brands of your favourite foods are and aren't vegan. By the end of the month I felt very differently about vegan food (I became totally accustomed to non-dairy milk in tea, for example – when the trial was up, I could hardly tell the difference... Honestly!).

3. Avoid 'fake' meat and cheese substitutes for a while. There are so many vegan meat and cheese substitutes out there that it is tempting to think you can eat pretty much the same food as before, just replacing your sausages or cheese with vegan lookalikes. First off, I think you will be disappointed. Most of these substitutes have quite a different texture and flavour to the real thing, and may well leave you feeling hard done by. Instead, try to cook without them for at least a month or two, then gradually try the various products on the market, working out which you like and which you don't.

4. Expect occasional 'wobbles'. Have a few favourite comfort food recipes on standby for when you're tempted to go astray. These needn't be 'fake' versions of whatever it is you're missing, but quick and really lip-smackingly tasty options that will distract you.

When I was craving a gooey, cheesey pasta bake in my first few weeks of veganism, I found that a spicy, creamy Thai green curry totally took my mind off it and reminded me what was great about what I could eat, rather than what I couldn't.

5. Plan ahead. Planning all your meals in advance for the first few weeks makes such a difference, and gets you into the right habits from the start. Finding vegan food on the go is one of the hardest aspects of the diet, so making up packed lunches and snacks for those first few weeks will help you stay on track.

Cooking Vegan

Vegan food is not difficult or time-consuming to prepare, it just takes a bit of a shift in how you think about cooking.

A great place to start is to look for simple recipes from cuisines which do vegan really well: Indian, Middle-Eastern, Thai, even Italian – many of their dishes are in fact 'accidentally' vegan, and taste fantastic. Once you're confident in the kitchen with some vegan recipes under your belt, you can experiment with vegan-ising your favourite recipes by making some simple substitutions.

• When you need to drop an ingredient, think about what that ingredient actually adds to a recipe. For instance, cheese: perhaps it's the saltiness or creaminess of the cheese that you're looking for, or a crispy topping. In which case more salt or stock, a little dairy-free cream, a splash of olive oil or a breadcrumb topping might work instead. Or chorizo: it may be the smoky spice, the kick of chilli, or simply the texture and crunch you like – so a pinch of smoked paprika and chilli flakes, extra salt, or some croutons or toasted pine nuts will probably make a good substitute.

• Many dairy-free products replace their dairy equivalents very easily. In most recipes:

– Dairy-free spread makes a great substitute for butter. Many supermarkets now stock some lovely spreads based on avocado oil, coconut oil or rapeseed oil, which are surprisingly 'buttery'.
– Soya, nut or oat creams work well in place of single cream (they won't whip or thicken, but are great in sauces, soups, curries, etc).
– Dairy-free milk can be used instead of milk in pretty much any recipe (even fairly technical baking recipes), and is great for brushing over pastry as a glaze.

• Egg substitutes can be a little trickier, but there are lots of options, it is just a case of working out what the egg is doing in the original recipe. The substitutions I use most often are ground chia or flax seeds mixed with water (in most cakes and biscuits), a powdered egg replacer which is now widely available in supermarkets or mashed banana or apple sauce (in pancakes, waffles or brownies). Incidentally, 'aquafaba', the water that chickpeas are cooked in, makes a lovely substitute for egg whites in many recipes. Search the web for more on vegan egg substitutes and you'll soon be an expert.

• Cheese substitutes are various, and all have their uses, but don't expect to be serving them on a cheeseboard if you're a cheese connoisseur. I've found some that are great for melting and using in sauces; an excellent vegan parmesan; and some soft cheeses which are good for no-bake cheesecakes or cream-cheese icing for cakes.

  – A great tip for re-creating a 'cheesy' flavour in sauces and soups is a rather bizarre ingredient called 'Nutritional Yeast Flakes'. These look a bit like fish food, but will make any white sauce, pesto or soup taste incredibly cheesy; what's more, they are fortified with the elusive vitamin B12 so are good for you too.

• Most brands of ready-made pastry (both shortcrust and puff) are made with vegetable fats – but, as ever, check the label to be sure.

Shopping Vegan

When I first started shopping vegan I was amazed to discover how many everyday groceries contain milk or egg powder. For me, these were some of the most important items to remove from my shopping list – egg and milk powder are very rarely from free-range or high-welfare sources, so by buying them a lot of people who might consider themselves ethical consumers are actually supporting the sort of factory farms they would be appalled about buying a packet of eggs from.

There are several brands out there which make egg-, milk- or butter-free versions of many everyday groceries. Once you've found them you will no longer need to do the label-reading routine, so shopping becomes considerably quicker as you go along. For example, while egg noodles obviously contain egg powder, the wholewheat equivalents by the same brands are very often egg-free, so a small switch is all that's needed to vegan-ise your favourite noodle dishes.

Herewith some other pointers to help you veganise your shopping:

• There are a few products where the lack of a vegan version might surprise you – for me one of these, until recently, was ready-made naan bread. A curry is one of my go-to options for a vegan feast for friends, with rice, poppadoms, bhajis, mango chutney and all the trimmings, but I could never find a naan bread that didn't contain just a smidgen of milk powder or a little butter. I got used to making my own in big batches and freezing it for when I needed it. I can now happily reveal, however, that Asda has brought out their own vegan naan, and pretty good it is too.

• When you are starting out, you may find shopping online preferable – ingredient lists are easier to read on-screen in a good-sized font, and it is much nicer to do this from the comfort of your sofa with a glass of (vegan) wine in hand, rather than squinting at the back of packets in a supermarket aisle with an impatient toddler in the trolley. It does take a bit of time at first, but you soon get to know which brands to use and which not.

• Make a list somewhere of your favourite brands (scribble them in the margins of recipes), and shopping will get quicker and easier every time. Some online supermarkets let you add products as a 'favourite', which is really handy for next time.

• Just because something isn't labelled as vegan doesn't mean it is off the menu. At first I assumed if something was labelled 'suitable for vegetarians' it probably wasn't vegan-friendly (or else why wouldn't they say so?); in fact, frustratingly, that's just not the case.

If in doubt, I've often found a quick internet search for 'is *** vegan?' to be successful – there are many useful forums and websites with up to date information, and sometimes the manufacturers' own websites are very helpful.

• A number of excellent vegan products and substitutes aren't yet available in mainstream supermarkets, so occasional trips to health-food shops or their online equivalents are always worthwhile.

• Throughout this book I've put this symbol ⟨CHECK⟩ next to any products, in particular, for which you will need to read the label – i.e. those which sometimes contain animal products, but for which many vegan versions are also available.

Stocking the Store Cupboard

This is a list of the dry/cupboard and fresh ingredients you will need to cook all the recipes in this book. If you are making the transition to a vegan diet, a spring-clean of your cupboards to make way for these staples would be a great way to start, and will make sure a delicious vegan meal is always just 15 minutes away.

For further information and to speed up your shopping, take a look at the 'Vegan Store Cupboard: Recommended Ingredients' page on my blog (www.thevegspace.co.uk/vegan-store-cupboard) where I try to keep an up to date list of which brands are vegan in each category.

N.B. This list is intended as a guide only. Always read the label carefully to check whether a product is vegan, and if you are uncertain or have any concerns, contact the manufacturer.

Baking Supplies:

Chickpea (gram) flour
Cocoa powder
Custard powder -(CHECK)
Dried apricots
Golden syrup
Maple syrup
Sugars (caster, icing,
  demerara and light brown)
Plain/dark chocolate -(CHECK)
Plain/dark choc chips -(CHECK)
Plain flour
Porridge oats
Self-raising flour
Vanilla extract

Dried Herbs & Spices:

Chinese five spice
Curry powder
Garam masala
Ground cinnamon
Ground cumin
Oregano
Paprika & smoked paprika
Turmeric
Za'tar

Dried pasta & noodles:

Mini-shells or
other small soup pasta -(CHECK)
Fusilli -(CHECK)
Linguine -(CHECK)
Macaroni -(CHECK)
Orzo -(CHECK)
Tagliatelle -(CHECK)
Fine & flat rice noodles
Soba noodles
Wholewheat noodles -(CHECK)

Jars:

Artichoke hearts
Ready-chopped garlic / garlic
  purée
Ready-chopped ginger /
  purée
Vegan mayonnaise
Passata (plain, with basil, and
  with onion and garlic)
Peanut butter (crunchy)
Preserved lemons
Sun-dried tomatoes
Dijon or English Mustard
Wholegrain Mustard
Capers
Gherkins
Olives (black and green,
  pitted)
Roasted peppers
Sliced Jalapeños

Alcohol:
Amaretto —(CHECK)
Dry sherry —(CHECK)
Red wine —(CHECK)
White wine —(CHECK)

Nuts & Seeds:
Almonds (whole and flaked)
Hazelnuts
Cashews
Pine nuts
Shelled pistachios
Peanuts (dry roasted and
  chilli-coated)
Pumpkin seeds
Sesame seeds
Walnut pieces
Sunflower seeds
Ground flax and/or chia
  seeds

Oils:
Coconut
Extra virgin olive
Olive
Rapeseed
Sesame
Sunflower

Vinegars:
Balsamic
White wine
Cider

Pastes:
Chipotle paste
Harissa
Vegan pesto
Curry pastes (korma and
  rogan josh)
Tahini
Thai curry paste (green or
  red) —(CHECK)
Tomato purée

Rice, Grains & Pulses:
Couscous
Freekeh (pre-cooked pouch)
Puy lentils (pre-cooked
  pouch)
Quick-cook polenta
Quinoa
Rice, pre-cooked in pouches
  (basmati, brown, long grain,
  pilau, thai jasmine)
Spelt (pre-cooked pouch)
Wholewheat giant
  couscous

Sauces:
Black bean
Brown
Soy
Sweet chilli
Tomato ketchup

Tinned Foods:
Baked beans
Chickpeas
Chopped tomatoes
Lentils (green)
Coconut Milk
Beans (borlotti, black beans,
  butter beans, haricot,
  cannellini)
Refried beans
Sweetcorn

Milks, Cream & Cheese Substitutes:
Dairy-free milks (soya,
  almond, hazelnut, cashew,
  oat, rice, coconut or hemp
  milk)
Dairy-free spread
Ready-made soya or oat
  custard
Vegan parmesan

Vegan cream cheese

Miscellaneous:
Vegetable stock (cubes and
  powder)
Nutritional yeast flakes
  (fortified with vitamin B12)
Spring roll wrappers
Dried porcini mushrooms
Oreo cookies
Silken tofu

In the Freezer:
Dairy-free vanilla ice cream
Peas
Broad beans
Spicy Thai mix
Char-grilled aubergine
Summer fruits
Breadcrumbs

On the Windowsill or in the Garden:
Flat-leaf parsley
Coriander
Basil
Thyme
Mint

Equipment:

Food processor or blender

Stick blender and mini-chopper

Microwave

Kettle

Frying pans (large and small)

Lidded saucepans (large and small)

Non-stick baking trays

Sharp knives (at least one large chef's knife, small paring knife, serrated bread knife)

Chopping board

Mixing bowls

Colander

Sieve

Tongs

Spatula

Slotted spoon

Peeler

Grater

Measuring jug

Measuring spoons

Scales

Tin opener

Rolling pin

Corkscrew & bottle opener

Nutrition: Practical Ideas

One of the first things that happens when you decide to go vegan is that everyone is suddenly very concerned about your nutrition (far more so than if you were living on a diet of turkey twizzlers and chips!):

Where on earth will you get your protein and calcium from?

But surely it's not healthy. Meat and fish are one thing, but you can't live without eggs and cheese...

This is simply not the case, and in fact there have been some pretty high-profile studies recently to show just how beneficial to your overall health a vegan diet can be. But of course you do need to keep an eye on certain aspects of your diet (just as you should whatever your dietary choices).

As you become experienced in eating vegan you will gain confidence in the fact that a balanced diet of

31

a variety of plant-based foods contains quite enough of the essential vitamins and minerals we all need to stay in optimum health. But if you are at all concerned, either when you are starting out or because you are not the sort of person who pays attention to detail in this way, I recommend that you take a specialist vegan multi-vitamin each day. Lots of vegans do.

I am not a qualified nutritionist, but I can offer some practical tips based on my own experience. The top five nutrients to keep an eye on are:

Protein – this is actually present in almost all plant-based foods, but particularly rich in beans, lentils, peas, soya (including tofu, milks and cheeses, tempeh, etc), nuts, seeds, grains (including quinoa, buckwheat, and even wholewheat bread and pasta). I try to make sure there's something protein-rich in every meal: for breakfast perhaps peanut butter, nut milk on cereal, or a handful of cashews or seeds in a banana smoothie; for lunch, baked beans, hummus, falafel or a sprinkle of pumpkin seeds over a salad; for a main meal, a dish incorporating beans, lentils or tofu, or some nuts and seeds in a pesto or a crispy breadcrumb topping. Eating enough protein really isn't the drama it is made out to be, but is worth bearing in mind when meal planning.

Vitamin B12 – this nutrient is found primarily in animal products like meat, fish, dairy and eggs, so vegans can be susceptible to a deficiency in it. But have no fear! There are a number of vegan foods which provide vitamin B12, including nutritional yeast flakes (see p22) and Marmite. Many dairy-free milks are fortified with B12, as are some breakfast cereals. But, as I have said, to be sure you are getting your recommended daily amount, you may wish to take a vegan multivitamin supplement.

Omega 3 and Omega 6 – these essential fats are found in a variety of nuts and seeds. I've found that a really simple way of upping omega 3 intake is to use rapeseed oil as a main cooking oil (many cheap oils labelled 'vegetable oil' are in fact 100% rapeseed oil so you don't need to spend a fortune on the cold-pressed stuff). Omega 3 is also found in ground flax seeds and chia seeds, which are a brilliant egg substitute in baking, as well as walnuts and hemp seeds (hemp seed oil makes lovely salad dressings). Omega 6 is found in nuts and seeds, sunflower oil and hemp oil. There are also many omega oil supplements on the market.

Calcium – lots of fabulous vegan ingredients are rich in calcium, including green leafy vegetables (kale, broccoli, rocket, watercress, spring greens, cabbage, etc), fortified soya and nut milks, nuts and seeds, kidney and black-eyed beans, chick-peas, tahini and many more.

Iron – getting enough iron in a vegan diet is very easy. In fact the average iron intake of vegans is usually the same if not higher than non-vegans. Iron-rich foods include wholegrains (including bread), pulses, leafy green vegetables, dried fruits and nuts and seeds.

For more detailed nutritional advice, the Vegan Society's website and Veganuary.com are packed with helpful and up-to-date information.

Tips for Quick Cooking

One of the key purposes of this book is to demonstrate that going vegan is not a laborious enterprise which might eat into your precious down time. There is, of course, no onus on you to prove the 15-minute rule just for the sake of it. But for those of you who like to know that you can have lunch or supper on the table at speed, here are a few useful tips.

• Preparation is key to cooking anything fast – you will need to start with your kettle filled and boiled (where necessary), and all the ingredients and equipment you need laid out on the worktop and ready to go.

• Don't faff around with scales! Where weights are specified, you can usually guesstimate from the size of the packet (e.g. 50g spinach is roughly half a 100g bag). I've used tablespoon measures rather than weights as often as possible for anything that needs a little more accuracy.

• It's worth noting that cooking time is very dependent on what sort of hob you are using. An induction or gas hob will speed up cooking considerably compared with an electric hob, which is slower to heat up and to react to changes you make. Whenever I find myself having to cook on electric, I tend to turn on at least one ring up high before I start, so that they are ready to go when I need them.

• A few pieces of equipment are fairly vital to efficient food prep and, if you don't have many kitchen gadgets, the one I would suggest investing in above all others is a mini chopper and hand blender set. There are some very reasonably priced ones on the market these days (under £25), and it will make a huge difference to your cooking.

• I've used quite a number of time-saving and convenience ingredients for the recipes here. They are usually a little more expensive than the uncooked alternative, so if you're on a budget and have a bit of time to spare, do cook your own rice, spelt, lentils, aubergines etc, or even cook in bulk and freeze individual portions.

EASY BRUNCH

Creamy Peach Breakfast Smoothie
Serves 1

Fruit smoothies are such a great way to start the day – packing in a good proportion of your five-a-day. I always add oats as I like a thicker consistency and find they keep me full for longer. A handful of almonds provides a great protein boost, while the flax or chia seeds with their omega oils turn this into a super-smoothie!

1 peach
1 banana
3 tbsp oats
2 tbsp whole almonds
250ml dairy-free milk (I use almond)
1 tsp ground flax or chia seeds (optional)

1. Remove the stone from the peach (no need to peel), and peel the banana.

2. Place all the ingredients in a blender and blitz until completely smooth (this will take 45-60 seconds on high speed). Pour into a glass and enjoy.

Griddled Asparagus with Lemony Sauce on Crumpets
Serves 1

The peppery, lemony sauce and asparagus are a perfect match, and I can't think of a better base than toasted crumpets, with all those little holes soaking up the sauce. A lazy weekend breakfast which takes minutes to throw together, and tastes totally indulgent.

2 tsp dairy-free spread
1 tsp plain flour
125ml dairy-free milk (soya, nut or oat)
Zest of 1 lemon
Rapeseed or sunflower oil
60g fine asparagus spears
2 crumpets CHECK

1. Melt the spread in a small saucepan and stir in the flour.

2. Add the milk a little at a time, and bring to a gentle boil, stirring constantly. Reduce to a simmer and cook for 2-3 minutes until it thickens. Season, grate in the lemon zest and remove from the heat.

3. Heat a drizzle of oil in a small frying pan, add the asparagus spears and cook for 2-3 minutes until turning brown and just tender.

4. Toast the crumpets, then top with the asparagus and pour over the sauce.

Blackberry Ripple Yoghurt Pots with Almond Crunch
Serves 2

These make a delicious breakfast but they are great, too, as an after-dinner treat. You can use any seasonal fruit – raspberries, strawberries or blackcurrants.

2 tbsp flaked almonds
2 tbsp jumbo oats
1 tbsp pumpkin seeds
1 tsp sunflower or coconut oil
1-2 tbsp maple syrup
1 tbsp apple juice
200g fresh blackberries
250g dairy-free yoghurt (coconut, almond or soya)

1. Toast the almonds in a dry frying pan over a medium heat for 1 minute. Stir in the oats and pumpkin seeds and toast for a further minute.

2. Add the oil and stir until evenly coated, then pour in the maple syrup and apple juice, stirring continuously for another minute or so, until the syrup has bubbled away, then tip onto a plate to cool.

3. Tip the blackberries into a bowl with a dash of extra maple syrup, and mash roughly with a fork.

4. Swirl the berry coulis through the yoghurt, and sprinkle over the almond crunch.

Smoky 'Full English' on Toast
Serves 1

A tasty treat for a hearty breakfast – all the best elements of a vegan 'Full English' cooked in one pot with a hint of smoky spices, served on crisp slices of toast.

Rapeseed or sunflower oil
1 vegan sausage
1 tomato
2 mushrooms (chestnut or closed-cup)
½ tsp ground cumin
½ tsp smoked paprika
200g tin baked beans
1 large or 2 small slices bread CHECK

1. Heat a drizzle of oil in a frying pan. Slice the sausage diagonally into 5 or 6 pieces, and fry them until both sides are starting to brown.

2. Quarter the tomato and mushrooms and add to the pan. Cook for 3-4 minutes until they begin to colour, then sprinkle over the cumin and paprika and stir well before pouring in the baked beans. Continue to cook for 2 minutes until the beans are piping hot and the sauce has reduced a little.

3. Toast the bread, then serve it topped with the 'Full English' beans.

Banana and Pecan Pancakes with Maple Syrup
Makes 8-9 small pancakes

Pancakes are too good to save for Shrove Tuesday, and these fluffy little banana ones are a treat for breakfast or brunch.

The banana acts as an egg-replacer here and makes these fairly moist, so they may need a little more cooking than traditional pancakes. They are at their best eaten straight away.

1 banana
150ml dairy-free milk (nut, oat or soya)
120g self-raising flour
1 tsp maple syrup (plus extra for drizzling)
Pinch of salt
3 tbsp sultanas
2 tbsp pecan nuts
Coconut oil or dairy-free margarine for frying

1. In a blender or food processor, blitz the banana, milk, flour, maple syrup and salt into a smooth batter. Pour it into a jug.

2. Roughly chop the pecan nuts, and stir them into the batter along with the sultanas.

3. Heat a little oil or margarine in a large frying pan, and pour the batter into three separate circles to create small pancakes. Fry gently for a minute or so until golden brown, then flip over and cook for a

further minute. Repeat this until all the batter has been used up.

4. Serve immediately, with a drizzle of maple syrup.

Smashed Avocado on Toast with Crispy Spring Onions and Chilli Yoghurt
Serves 2

I know, avocado toast is a bit of a cliché when it comes to vegan breakfast ideas, but this extra-special version with crispy spring onions and chilli yoghurt is definitely worthy of inclusion here as a seriously tasty way to start the day.

Charred spring onions are delicious – I often pop a few around the edges of a barbecue to add to veggie burgers, sausages or grilled vegetable feasts.

4 spring onions
Rapeseed or sunflower oil
1 ripe avocado
Half a lemon
Half a red chilli
1 tbsp dairy-free yoghurt (coconut or soya)
2 slices crusty, thickly sliced bread ─CHECK⟩

1. Trim the spring onions, and halve lengthways. Heat a drizzle of oil in a griddle or frying pan, and throw in the onions. Cook them until brown and crispy, about 2 minutes per side, then remove the pan from the heat.

2. Scoop the avocado flesh into a small bowl, then add the lemon juice and a sprinkle of salt and pepper. Mash the mixture roughly with a fork until combined.

3. De-seed and finely chop the chilli, tip it into a mug or small bowl and mix in the dairy-free yoghurt. Season to taste.

4. Toast the bread, then top each slice with half the avocado mixture, four spring onion halves, and a drizzle of the chilli yoghurt.

Bubble and Squeak Fry-up with Grilled Tomatoes
Serves 2

Bubble and squeak is one of life's simple pleasures, and this speedy fry-up is just as good for dinner, perhaps alongside some vegan sausages, as it is for brunch.

1 floury potato
1 medium parsnip
2 tomatoes
2 tbsp rapeseed or sunflower oil
1 onion
4-5 large leaves savoy cabbage
Knob dairy-free spread
Nutmeg

1. Preheat the grill to its highest setting.

2. Peel the potato and parsnip and chop them into 1cm cubes.

3. Tip them into a saucepan of salted boiling water, and boil for 5-6 minutes until they are almost cooked through. Drain them and set them aside in a sieve or colander so that they dry out as much as possible.

4. Meanwhile, halve the tomatoes, spray or rub them with a little oil and salt and pepper, then grill them until golden brown.

5. Remove the woody stalks from the centre of the cabbage leaves, then roll the leaves up into a tube to

slice them very finely. Peel and finely chop the onion.

6. Heat the oil in a large frying pan, add the onion and cabbage and cook them on a high heat for 2 minutes until starting to soften. Add the potatoes and parsnips, season well and continue cooking. After 2-3 minutes, add the dairy-free spread and a grating of nutmeg, then cook for a further 3-4 minutes until everything is just turning golden brown.

7. Serve the bubble and squeak with the grilled tomatoes nestling on top.

Hazelnut and Plum Porridge with Pumpkin Seeds
Serves 1

Porridge made with hazelnut milk isn't going to win any beauty pageant prizes. However it more than makes up for its slightly murky colour with its creaminess and nutty flavour – do give it a try.

Toasting the oats in the dry saucepan for just a minute before adding the milk is my top tip for making porridge taste even more porridgey. Delicious and good for you too.

50g porridge oats
200ml hazelnut milk (or any other dairy-free milk works well here)
Pinch of salt
½ tsp demerara sugar
1 plum, destoned and halved
1 tbsp pumpkin seeds
5-6 hazelnuts

1. Tip the oats into a dry saucepan and toast them over a medium heat for 1 minute, stirring frequently.

2. Pour in the hazelnut milk, and bring it to the boil. Add the salt and sugar, then finely chop one half of the plum and add this to the porridge too.

3. Cook, stirring constantly, for 5-6 minutes until you have a thick, creamy consistency. If the porridge

looks a little dry, add a splash more hazelnut milk. Taste and add a pinch more sugar if required.

4. When the porridge is ready, tip it into a bowl. Slice the remaining half plum, arranging the pieces on top. Roughly chop the hazelnuts and scatter them over the porridge followed by the pumpkin seeds. Eat immediately.

SPEEDY SOUPS

Chunky Green Minestrone with Curly Kale

Serves 2 as a main or 4 as a starter

This gloriously green soup is a meal in itself. The beauty of using frozen peas and broad beans is that you can enjoy the taste of spring at any time of year.

1 leek
2 tbsp rapeseed or sunflower oil
1 tsp ready-chopped garlic / garlic purée
4 small new potatoes
1 litre boiling water
5 tbsp soup pasta (mini shells, small macaroni or broken spaghetti -CHECK
5 tbsp frozen peas
5 tbsp broad beans
1 vegetable stock cube -CHECK
2 large handfuls curly kale
Handful fresh parsley

1. Heat the oil in a large saucepan or casserole. Finely slice the leek and add it to the pan, followed by the garlic. Cook for 2 minutes until starting to soften.

2. Meanwhile, finely slice the new potatoes into rounds ½cm thick (no need to peel).

3. Pour the boiling water into the saucepan, and add the potatoes, pasta, peas, broad beans, stock cube, a small pinch of salt and black pepper. Turn up the heat to bring it to the boil and be sure to keep the heat

high – the pasta and potatoes need a good 10 minutes of cooking time (and adding frozen things to boiling water makes the temperature plummet for a while).

4. While this is cooking, remove any woody stalks from the kale and slice it finely. Remove the stalks from the parsley and finely chop the leaves.

5. About 5 minutes into the cooking time, add the curly kale to the pan.

6. When the pasta is cooked through, use a hand blender to part-blend the soup (you are aiming to thicken it, not to purée the whole lot). Alternatively, pour about a quarter of the soup into a blender or food processor and blitz it until smooth, then return it to the pan.

7. Stir through the parsley, and add more salt and pepper if needed.

Thai Sweet Potato and Coconut Soup
Serves 2 as a main or 4 as a starter

A mini-chopper or food processor is your friend here – it will blitz the raw ingredients into tiny pieces so they cook through quickly.

If you don't have any of these kitchen gadgets, you can chop the veg by hand, but you will need to add an extra 5-10 minutes to the cooking time.

2 tbsp rapeseed or sunflower oil
2 tbsp red Thai curry paste ⟨CHECK⟩ (some contain fish sauce)
1 onion
1 large or 2 small carrots
2 medium sweet potatoes
400ml tin reduced fat coconut milk
1 tsp vegetable stock powder ⟨CHECK⟩
Handful fresh coriander leaves

1. Heat the oil and curry paste in a large saucepan. Peel and quarter the onion, blitz it in a mini-chopper or food processor, add it to the saucepan and stir.

2. Peel the carrots and sweet potatoes. Cut each into large chunks, then blitz into very small pieces (either all at once in a larger food processor, or one by one in a mini-chopper). Add them to the pan and stir well.

3. Turn the heat up high and pour in the coconut milk. Re-fill the empty tin with water, and add this to the pan. Bring it to the boil as quickly as you can,

adding the stock powder and a generous seasoning of salt as you go.

4. Simmer vigorously for 10 minutes, then at the last minute, use a hand blender to blitz to a very smooth soup. Add the coriander leaves and blitz once more so that they are finely mixed through. Season to taste and serve.

Oyster Mushroom Tom Yum Soup with Rice Noodles
Serves 2

Please don't think this clear soup is in any way bland or watery. It is jam-packed with flavour and, while not particularly authentic to a Tom Yum recipe, I've added rice noodles to turn it into a more substantial dish. Alternatively, it is lovely with some cooked jasmine rice stirred through. Don't skimp on the chilli or lime juice – Tom Yum needs to be both hot and sour, and you won't regret being generous with either.

2 tbsp rapeseed or sunflower oil
1½ tbsp red Thai curry paste –CHECK
50g fine rice noodles
1 medium shallot (banana or echalion)
1 red chilli
125g oyster mushrooms
800ml boiling water
1 tsp vegetable stock powder –CHECK
1 tsp sugar
1 tbsp tomato purée
2 spring onions
Small bunch coriander
1 lime

1. Heat the oil in a large saucepan or casserole, stir in the Thai curry paste and cook over a medium heat.

2. Put the rice noodles in a heatproof bowl or jug,

cover them with boiling water, and leave them to soak for 8-10 minutes until soft.

3. De-seed the chilli and finely slice it with the shallot and add them both to the pan. Halve or roughly slice the oyster mushrooms and tip these in too.

4. After cooking the vegetables vigorously for 2 minutes, pour in the boiling water, followed by the stock powder, tomato purée, and sugar. Season with salt and bring to the boil. Trim and slice the spring onions and add them to the soup. Cook for 3-4 minutes.

5. Roughly chop the coriander leaves (discard the stalks), and stir them through the soup at the last minute. Taste and add a little more salt if required.

6. Drain the noodles and rinse them under cold water. Divide the noodles between two bowls, and pour the soup over the top. Squeeze the juice of half a lime over each bowl, and serve.

Top Tip: One of my favourite 'cheat' ingredients is something you can buy in a packet from Waitrose – Spicy Thai Mix – a frozen blend of chopped herbs, garlic and chilli which makes an excellent base for this hot and sour soup.

Creamy Sweetcorn and Chilli Chowder with Quick Garlic Bread
Serves 4

As warming bowls of soup go, this chowder is hard to beat. The garlic bread takes minutes under a hot grill and is ideal for dunking.

For the chowder:
2 tbsp rapeseed or sunflower oil
1 onion
1 tsp ready-chopped garlic /garlic purée
1 heaped tsp plain flour
600ml nut or soya milk
250ml boiling water
1 vegetable stock cube ⌐CHECK⊐
1 medium potato
1 red chilli
400g tinned sweetcorn
6-8 fresh chives

For the garlic bread:
4 slices crusty baguette ⌐CHECK⊐
2 tbsp dairy-free spread
1 tsp ready-chopped garlic /garlic purée
4 chives

1. Pre-heat the grill to its highest setting.

2. Heat the oil in a large saucepan or casserole. Peel and chop the onion, and add it to the pan followed by the garlic.

3. After 1 minute, stir through the flour, then pour in the milk, water and stock cube. Bring to the boil as quickly as possible.

4. Peel and grate the potato and add it to the pan. De-seed and finely slice the chilli and drain the sweetcorn and tip both of these into the soup, then season well with salt and black pepper.

5. While the soup is bubbling, mash together the dairy-free spread and garlic for the garlic bread topping in a mug or small bowl, then chop in the chives with a clean pair of scissors and mix. Lay the bread slices on the grill pan and cover each one generously with the garlic spread. Place under the grill and watch carefully – it can quickly burn.

6. Use a hand blender to purée the soup until completely smooth (this may take 40–50 seconds, so keep going). Taste and adjust seasoning, then serve with any remaining chives snipped on top, and the garlic bread on the side.

Gently Curried Lentil Soup
Serves 2 as a main or 4 as a starter

A steaming flask or bowl of this spicy, lemony lentil soup is wonderful on a chilly winter lunchtime – and it is super-quick to make thanks to the tinned lentils.

Lentil soup, like most soups, curries and stews, is even better the following day once the flavours have had time to mingle properly, so make sure you leave a portion in the fridge for tomorrow's lunch.

2 tbsp rapeseed or sunflower oil
1 onion
2 carrots
2 tsp mild curry powder
1 tsp ready-chopped garlic / garlic purée
1 tsp ready-chopped ginger / ginger purée
400g tin green lentils
750ml boiling water
1 vegetable stock cube CHECK
Juice of ½ lemon
Handful spinach leaves

1. Roughly cut up the onion and carrots and use a food processor to chop them finely.

2. Heat the oil in a large, lidded saucepan or casserole on a fairly high heat. Add the finely chopped onion and carrots.

3. Put the curry powder, ginger and garlic into the pan

and stir to combine everything. Cook for 2 minutes until it starts to turn soft.

4. Meanwhile, boil the kettle, drain and rinse the lentils and tip them, the boiling water and the stock cube into the pan. Cover the saucepan and cook on a high heat, bubbling vigorously for 10 minutes.

5. Remove from the heat, then add the lemon juice and spinach, and use a hand blender to blitz until smooth. Taste and adjust the seasoning if necessary.

Tuscan Borlotti Bean Soup with Orzo
Serves 4

This thick, beany soup, packed with tiny orzo pasta, as well as vegetables and beans, is a meal in itself. Serve it with a hunk of crusty bread or perhaps some sourdough croutons.

2 tbsp rapeseed or sunflower oil
1 onion
1 carrot
1 stick celery
1 tsp ready-chopped garlic / garlic purée
1 tsp smoked paprika
1 litre boiling water
1 vegetable stock cube ⌐CHECK⌐
3 tbsp tomato purée
70g orzo (or other very small pasta shape) ⌐CHECK⌐
400g tin borlotti beans
2 leaves savoy cabbage or a handful curly kale

1. Heat the oil in a large saucepan or casserole. Peel the onion, and slice it into quarters. Peel the carrot, top and tail the celery, and slice both into large chunks. Use a mini-chopper or food processor to blitz the onion, carrot and celery into very small pieces, then tip them all into the saucepan. Add the garlic and smoked paprika, stir and cook on a high heat for 2-3 minutes.

2. Pour in the boiling water, then add the stock cube,

tomato purée and orzo. Drain and rinse the borlotti beans and put them in the soup, then season well with salt and black pepper. Bring to the boil before reducing it to a medium heat and simmer for 5 minutes.

3. Remove any tough stalks from the cabbage or kale, and slice it finely. Add it to the soup then simmer for a further 5 minutes until the orzo is cooked through.

4. When the soup is cooked, remove it from the heat, and use a hand blender to blitz it for a few short pulses, to slightly thicken it. Alternatively, blitz a quarter of the soup in a blender then return it to the pan. Taste and adjust the seasoning if required.

Mixed Mushroom Curry Laksa
Serves 2

Laksa is a dish from Indonesia and Malaysia, based on rice noodles served in a spicy coconut soup. There are all sorts of variations, but the addition of both Thai spices and Indian curry powder is traditional, influenced by the various trading routes and spice merchants in the region.

I like to pack my Laksa with mushrooms and noodles to turn it into a delicious main course. This version is fairly spicy – leave out the chilli or use less of the Thai ingredients mix for a less fiery alternative!

75g fine rice noodles
2 tbsp rapeseed or sunflower oil
1 tbsp spicy Thai curry mix (see p59)
1 tsp curry powder
1 red chilli
Handful fresh coriander
120g mixed 'exotic' mushrooms
400g tin coconut milk
Handful beansprouts
Juice of 1 lime

1. Place the noodles in a heatproof jug or bowl, cover them in boiling water and leave them to soak for 10 minutes until soft.

2. Heat the oil in a large, deep frying pan, and stir in

the Thai curry mix. Sprinkle over the curry powder. Cook over a gentle heat so the spices release their flavours but do not burn.

3. Finely chop the stalks of the coriander (set aside the leaves for later), and de-seed and finely slice the chilli. Add both to the pan. Slice the mushrooms into bite-sized pieces and put them in the pan to cook for 2 minutes.

4. Pour in the coconut milk, then fill the empty tin about a third full with water and pour that into the pan too. Season well with salt, bring to the boil, then reduce the heat and simmer for 5-6 minutes.

5. Tip the beansprouts into the pan for the last minute of cooking time.

6. Drain the noodles and rinse them under cold water, then divide them between two serving dishes. Finely chop the coriander leaves and stir them through the coconut broth.

7. Remove the broth from the heat, squeeze over the lime juice and stir, then taste and add a little more salt if necessary. Pour the broth over the noodles and serve immediately.

SALADS

Spring Greens Giant Couscous with Avocado and Toasted Almonds
Serves 2

Is it a warm salad, a 'goodness bowl', a stir-fry or something else? I'm not really sure to be honest, but it makes a lovely healthy lunch, so tuck in!

Wholewheat giant couscous is infinitely more appealing than the non-wholewheat version, which when cooked seems to end up with a texture that a friend accurately describes as 'frogspawn'. Keep tasting it for the last few minutes of cooking so that you catch it when it is just al-dente, and still has a nutty bite.

150g wholewheat giant couscous
1 tsp vegetable stock powder -CHECK
3 tbsp whole almonds
200g spring greens
4 spring onions
2 tbsp olive oil
1 tsp ready-chopped garlic / garlic purée
Juice of 1 lemon
1 avocado

1. Fill a saucepan with boiling water, and tip in the couscous and stock powder. Bring to the boil and cook for 6-8 minutes until just tender. The grains should still have some bite to them.

2. Heat a large, dry frying pan over a fairly high heat and tip in the almonds. Toast them for a few minutes until the skins are starting to brown, then put them in a small bowl.

3. Remove the woody stalks from the spring greens, and slice the leaves very finely. Trim the spring onions and chop them into thin rounds.

4. Heat the oil in the frying pan, add the garlic, spring greens and spring onions, and season well. Cook for 2-3 minutes until the leaves are tender, then turn off the heat.

5. When the couscous is cooked, drain it and tip it into the frying pan with the spring greens. Stir to combine, then squeeze over the lemon juice.

6. Divide the couscous mix between two plates. De-stone the avocado and scoop out the flesh and pile it on top of the couscous. Roughly chop the toasted almonds and sprinkle these over, then serve.

Grilled Portobello & Cherry Tomato Panzanella
Serves 2

I never really got the point of the traditional Tuscan dish of panzanella – surely it was just soggy bread and tomatoes? Then I tried a really good one and realised how delicious this simple dish can be.

While this isn't an authentic panzanella recipe (mushrooms wouldn't usually get a look-in, and grilling some of the ingredients is probably a no-no in rural Tuscany), it has a lovely combination of textures – juicy pieces of mushroom and crisp ciabatta soaking up just enough of the dressing and tomato juices. Definitely a dinner to eat al fresco on a warm summer's evening.

2 large or 3 small Portobello mushrooms
12 cherry tomatoes
Half a red onion
Olive oil
Half a jar roasted peppers
8 green olives
1 tbsp capers
Handful fresh basil leaves
1 ciabatta roll (or 2 slices crusty bread) —(CHECK)

For the dressing:
1 tbsp extra virgin olive oil
2 tsp white wine vinegar
Pinch of sugar

1. Heat the grill to its highest setting. Cut the mushrooms into roughly 2cm chunks, halve the cherry tomatoes, and peel and slice the red onion. Place all in a bowl, drizzle with a little olive oil, season with salt and pepper and toss until everything is evenly coated. Tip the mixture onto a baking tray and place under the grill for 8 minutes.

2. Drain the peppers on kitchen paper, then slice them into thin strips. Halve the olives. Put them both in a large serving bowl, along with the capers. Chop the basil leaves and add them to the bowl.

3. In a mug, whisk the dressing ingredients together.

4. Cut or tear the ciabatta or bread into large chunks. When the vegetables have been grilling for 8 minutes, add the bread to the baking tray to toast slightly for 2 minutes. Finally, put the grilled vegetables and bread in the bowl with the olives and capers, toss everything together then add the dressing and mix well. Serve immediately.

Warm Puy Lentil Salad with Beetroot, Baby Spinach and Sun-Blush Tomatoes
Serves 2

This protein-packed salad makes a fantastic lunch bowl, or part of an al-fresco buffet table for a warm summer's day. I've also stuffed it in pittas, and used up leftovers as a jacket potato filling – oh so versatile!

These are the sorts of ingredients I tend to have hanging around in my fridge, but you can throw in anything you fancy – chopped hazelnuts or walnuts, cooked broccoli, stir-fried kale, lemon juice, or halved cherry tomatoes.

250g pouch ready-to-eat puy lentils (or tinned lentils, drained and rinsed).
2 cooked beetroots
6 sun-blush (or sun-dried) tomatoes in oil
Large handful baby spinach leaves
Small handful fresh parsley
2 tbsp pumpkin seeds
2 tbsp extra virgin olive oil
1 tbsp balsamic vinegar

1. Heat the lentils according to packet instructions, then tip them into a large bowl.

2. Halve and thinly slice the beetroot and add it to the bowl.

3. Lay the tomatoes on a piece of kitchen paper to

remove a little oil, then slice them finely and add them too.

4. Roughly chop the baby spinach leaves and the parsley and add both to the bowl, followed by the pumpkin seeds.

5. In a mug or small bowl, whisk together the olive oil, balsamic vinegar and a generous pinch of salt and black pepper. Pour the dressing into the bowl and mix all the ingredients together until fully coated. Taste and add a little more salt if required, then serve.

Bright Green Freekeh Salad
Serves 2

This summery salad, with its herby lemon dressing, is packed with interesting flavours.

Do substitute in whatever you happen to have to hand – this would be lovely with cooked beetroot, sun-dried tomatoes, cooked broad beans or leftover lentils.

250g pouch ready-to-eat freekeh
5 tbsp frozen (or fresh) peas
100g mange tout
2 spring onions
Half a cucumber
45g rocket
Handful fresh parsley leaves
Handful fresh mint leaves
4 tbsp extra-virgin olive oil
Juice of 1 lemon
2 tbsp water
2 tbsp pine nuts

1. Cook the freekeh pouch according to packet instructions. Tip into a large bowl to cool.

2. Pour boiling water into a small saucepan, and boil the peas for 3 minutes. Slice the mange tout in half diagonally, add them to the pan and boil for a further minute. Drain and add to the bowl with the freekeh.

3. Trim and finely slice the spring onions, cut the cucumber into 6 slices lengthways, then slice it into small chunks. Add these to the bowl, along with the rocket.

4. In a mini-chopper, blitz the parsley, mint, olive oil, lemon juice, salt, pepper and water to make a bright green dressing. Spoon this into the bowl and toss everything together until evenly coated.

5. Divide between two plates and scatter with the pine nuts.

Top Tip: If you can't get hold of ready-cooked freekeh, many other grains will work well here – try quinoa, spelt or even brown rice. Or if you can get hold of uncooked freekeh, cook a large batch and freeze it in individual portions for defrosting and then cook as above.

Crunchy Thai Vegetable and Peanut Salad
Serves 2 as a main or 4 as a side dish

This is a bright and fresh tasting dish, packed with raw vegetables and roasted peanuts. Perfect as a light lunch or a buffet dish or side salad for a barbecue.

For the salad:
6 mange tout
Half a red pepper
1 carrot
2 spring onions
1 red chilli
Handful fresh coriander
Handful beansprouts
25g peanuts

For the dressing:
Juice of 1 lime
2 tsp caster sugar
2 tsp soy sauce
2 tsp sesame oil
1 tbsp smooth peanut butter

1. Finely slice the mange tout and red pepper into long strips. Peel and slice the carrots into thin matchsticks. Trim and slice the spring onions, and de-seed and finely chop the chilli. Roughly chop the coriander and peanuts. Combine all these vegetables along with the beansprouts in a large bowl and mix.

2. Whisk all the dressing ingredients together and toss it through the vegetables, making sure everything gets a good coating.

Beetroot and Apple Salad with Walnuts and Yoghurt
Serves 2

This flavour-packed salad can be made at any time of year. It is both beautiful to look at and a treat to eat, with the bitterness of the walnuts offset by crisp apple and sweet shavings of beetroot.

Large handful mixed leaves (rocket, watercress, pea shoots, baby spinach)
2 tbsp dairy-free yoghurt
1 tsp Dijon mustard
Juice of 1 lemon
Half an apple
1 pre-cooked beetroot
2 tbsp walnut pieces
Fresh dill
Fresh cress

1. Arrange the mixed leaves on a large plate or divide between two plates as required.

2. To make the yoghurt dressing, mix together the dairy-free yoghurt, Dijon mustard, a generous pinch of salt and black pepper, and half of the lemon juice in a mug or small bowl.

3. Core the apple and slice it very finely (use a mandoline if you have one). Toss the slices in the remaining lemon juice to stop them turning brown,

then arrange them over the mixed leaves.

4. Slice the beetroot very finely, and place it on top of the apple.

5. Roughly chop the walnuts and scatter them over the beetroot, then sprinkle over the dill and cress. Drizzle with the yoghurt and mustard dressing, and serve immediately.

Tenderstem, Cucumber and Soba Noodle Salad
Serves 2

This noodle salad makes a delicious packed lunch. The stir-fried tenderstem broccoli stays crisp and crunchy even if kept in a lunchbox for a few hours, and the combination of peanut dressing and nutty soba noodles should keep you full until dinner time.

200g soba (buckwheat) noodles
2 tbsp rapeseed or sunflower oil
120g tenderstem broccoli tips
1 tsp ready-chopped garlic / garlic purée
1 tsp ready-chopped ginger / ginger purée
Half a cucumber
3 spring onions
1 tbsp sesame oil
1 tbsp soy sauce
4 tbsp water
2 tbsp crunchy peanut butter

1. Fill a large saucepan with boiling water, and add the noodles. Simmer for 5 minutes.

2. Meanwhile, slice the broccoli tips in half lengthways through the stalk. Heat the oil in a small frying pan and add the brocolli along with the ginger, garlic. Season well with salt, and cook it over a medium heat for 10 minutes, stirring regularly, until slightly charred and crispy.

3. When the noodles are cooked through, drain and rinse them thoroughly under cold running water. Tip them into a large bowl.

4. Use a potato peeler to shave off strips of cucumber (just the fleshy section, discard the seeds). Add this to the bowl with the noodles.

5. Slice the spring onions and add them to the bowl.

6. In a mug, whisk together the sesame oil, soy sauce, water and peanut butter with a fork to form a fairly smooth dressing. Pour it over the noodles, and toss through the salad.

7. When the broccoli is cooked through, divide the noodles between two plates (or lunchboxes) and top with the broccoli.

Speedy Spinach Falafel with Carrot and Apple Salad
Serves 2-3 (makes 9-10 falafels)

Yes, I know – spinach falafel with carrot and apple salad sounds a bit hippy vegan café, but these little beauties are tasty enough to justify a place at any table. Falafel are great food on the go, and you can pack them with all sorts of vegetables, nuts and seeds. For a bit of variation, try blitzing in a cooked beetroot and some curly kale or grated carrot before shaping the balls.

For the falafel:
1 chilli (red or green)
Large handful baby spinach
400g tin chickpeas
1 tbsp plain flour
½ tsp baking powder
1 tsp ground cumin
1 tsp ground coriander
1 tbsp olive oil
1 lemon
Sunflower oil for frying

For the salad:
2 carrots
1 apple
1 tbsp olive oil
Handful fresh coriander

1. De-seed the chilli, and place it in a food processor along with the spinach, chickpeas, flour, baking powder, cumin, ground coriander, olive oil and zest of the lemon, and season well with salt and pepper.

2. Blitz everything to a chunky paste, then scoop out golf-ball-sized pieces of the mixture, roll it into balls between your hands, and repeat until all of it has been used up – you should end up with 9 or 10 falafel.

3. Cover the bottom of a large frying pan with oil and place the pan on a high heat. Put the falafel into the pan and cook them for 5-6 minutes, turning occasionally and adjusting the heat so that they don't burn. When they are brown all over and cooked through, remove the falafel from the pan and place them on a piece of kitchen paper to drain any excess oil.

4. Whilst the falafel are cooking, peel the carrots and core the apple, and use a julienne cutter, spiraliser or a sharp knife to slice them both into long, thin matchsticks. Place in a large bowl.

5. In a mug or small bowl, whisk the olive oil with the juice of the lemon (which you zested earlier), season with salt and pepper and pour it over the carrot and apple. Finely chop the coriander and toss it through the salad, then top with the falafel and serve.

FAST LUNCH

Pitta Stuffed with Harissa Chickpeas and Hummus
Serves 2

Harissa is a North African red pepper and chilli paste – smoky, slightly spicy and fragrant with rose petals. It gives these quick and easy chickpeas a gentle warmth and exotic flavour.

2 tbsp rapeseed or sunflower oil
1 red onion
400g tin of chickpeas
1 tbsp tomato purée
1 tbsp harissa paste
200ml boiling water
1 level tsp vegetable stock powder -CHECK
Handful fresh coriander
2 large pitta breads
Half a small tub of hummus
Handful of rocket

1. Heat the oil in a frying pan. Peel and slice the onion and add it to the pan. Cook for 2 minutes until it starts to soften.

2. Drain and rinse the chickpeas and put them in the pan, followed by the tomato purée and harissa. Stir to coat everything evenly.

3. Add the water and stock powder, then bring to the boil and cook on a medium heat until the sauce has

spread liberally with passata, right to the edges. Finely slice the sun-dried tomatoes and scatter over the pizza.

3. Cut off all the stalks from the broccoli, leaving just very small florets. Remove the woody stems from the kale and roughly chop. Scatter the broccoli and kale over the pizza, followed by the pine nuts.

4. Drizzle with olive oil, sprinkle generously with oregano, then season well with salt and freshly ground black pepper.

5. Bake for 8 minutes, or until the broccoli and kale have turned golden brown and crispy.

Make it spicy: add slices of fresh chilli, or a generous pinch of chilli flakes before cooking, or drizzle with chilli oil just before serving.

Artichoke and Watercress Brown Rice Bowl with Pine Nuts
Serves 2

Brown rice, with its nutty flavour and slightly chewy texture, makes a delicious base for a warm salad.

Grilling cherry tomatoes like this effectively makes 'cheat's' slow-roast tomatoes, and squashing them with a fork halfway through cooking helps their juices to cook off so that the flavour really intensifies.

12 cherry tomatoes
250g pouch pre-cooked brown rice
3 spring onions
150g sliced artichoke hearts in oil
60g watercress
Large handful fresh parsley
1 lemon
2 tbsp extra virgin olive oil
3 tbsp pine nuts

1. Heat the grill to its highest setting. Halve the cherry tomatoes, and lay them cut-side up on a baking tray or grill pan lined with foil. Season well with salt and pepper and place under the grill. After 8 minutes, squash each tomato with a fork and return to the grill for a further 4 minutes.

2. Meanwhile, heat the rice according to the packet instructions, then put it in a large bowl to cool.

3. Trim and finely slice the spring onions, finely chop the parsley, roughly chop the watercress, and add all of them to the bowl.

4. Lay the artichoke slices on a piece of kitchen paper to drain excess oil, then gently stir these in.

5. Squeeze the juice of the lemon into the bowl, and add the olive oil, pine nuts and a generous seasoning of salt and pepper. Toss all the ingredients to combine.

6. When the tomatoes are starting to turn brown at the edges, tip them into the bowl along with any juices from the tray, and mix them through the rice. Divide it all between the two bowls and serve.

Top Tip: When using pouches of rice or grains as an ingredient, I tend to microwave them first before adding to the dish, as I find the grains can otherwise be difficult to separate. But if you're short on time or don't have a microwave, just throw it in – it will all work out fine in the end!

Speedy Bean Burger with Gherkins and Mustard Mayo

Serves 2

This must be the speediest vegan burger ever made, and quite possibly the tastiest. Spicy refried beans are a great 'cheat' ingredient as they are ready seasoned and full of punch.

When I first tried vegan mayonnaise I wasn't 100% sold on the flavour, so I always mixed it with strong-flavoured additions like mustard, pesto or chipotle paste. Years later, the habit has stuck, though if you prefer your mayo unflavoured do experiment as there are now many more vegan options on the market to choose from.

Handful fresh coriander leaves
215g tin spicy refried beans CHECK
2 tbsp breadcrumbs
Plain flour for dusting
1 tbsp rapeseed or sunflower oil
Half an onion
2 large or 4 small gherkins
1 tbsp vegan mayonnaise
1 tsp Dijon mustard
Handful fresh rocket leaves
2 seeded burger buns CHECK

1. Chop the coriander leaves very finely, and put them in a bowl with the refried beans and the breadcrumbs

These are recipes to lift your spirits
... and show you how deliciously
easy veganism can be

Banana and Pecan Pancakes with Maple Syrup p44

Bubble and Squeak p48; Lemony Asparagus on Crumpets p41
Sweetcorn Chilli Chowder p60; Creamy Mushroom Fusilli p138

Panzanella p72; Bright Green Freekah Salad p76
Tahini & Cashew Quinoa Bowl p136; Beetroot, Apple and Walnut p80

Speedy Bean Burger with Gherkin p96

Broccoli and Kale Pine Nut Pizza p92

Chickpea & Kale Curry p128; Savoy Sesame Noodles with Tofu p130; Cauliflower & Chard Spelt Risotto p126; One-Pot Linguine p124

Tenderstem and Kale with Butter Bean Mash p134
Peanut Vietnamese Rolls p108

Caramelised Peaches on French Toast p166;
Chocolate 'Freakshake' p170; Salted Caramel Chocolate Mousse p180

and mash everything together with a fork until fully combined. Divide the mixture in two on a floured chopping board or surface, and shape each half into a burger, sprinkling the top with a little flour too.

2. Heat the oil in a frying pan, and fry the burgers over a medium heat for 3-4 minutes on each side until golden brown and crispy. While they are cooking, peel and slice the onion and add it to the pan.

3. In a mug or small bowl, combine the mayonnaise and mustard, then finally slice the gherkins in half or into slices as you prefer.

4. To make up the burger, split the bun, place some rocket on the bottom, put the burger on top, spoon over the mayonnaise and onions, then add the sliced gherkins. Serve immediately.

Preserved Lemon and Apricot Couscous with Za'tar Almonds
Serves 2

This tasty couscous dish is packed with the flavours of North Africa. It makes a delicious lunchbox treat, or a perfect accompaniment to barbecued veggie burgers or grilled mushrooms.

4 dried apricots
8 pitted green olives
Half a red onion
250ml boiling water
1 tsp vegetable stock powder —CHECK
½ tsp ground cumin
½ tsp cinnamon
120g couscous
3 preserved lemons
1 tbsp olive oil
1 tsp za'tar
3 tbsp whole almonds
Handful flat-leaf parsley
Juice of half a lemon

1. Thinly slice the apricots, quarter the olives and peel and finely chop the onion.

2. Bring the water and stock powder to the boil in a saucepan, add the cumin, cinnamon, couscous, apricots, olives and onion. Stir well, then remove the pan from the heat and set it aside, lid on, for 10 minutes.

3. Quarter the preserved lemons, and remove and discard the inner flesh with a knife. Slice the peel into thin strips then add it to the pan with the couscous and stir.

4. Heat a small frying pan, and add a glug of oil, the za'tar and salt. Tip in the almonds and toast them until golden brown all over then remove from the heat.

5. Chop the parsley leaves and stir them through the couscous, then squeeze in the lemon juice and stir. Taste and add a little salt if necessary. Roughly chop the almonds and scatter them over the couscous just before serving.

Black Bean Tacos with Avocado and Roasted Peppers
Serves 2

Tacos are often associated with those rock-hard, pre-fried, U-shaped shells you can buy in kits, shrink-wrapped in plastic from the supermarket (can you tell I'm not a fan?). Toasting your own tortilla wrap into a 'shell' for stuffing is quick, satisfying and infinitely tastier.

1 tbsp rapeseed or sunflower oil
Half a red onion
1 tsp ready-chopped garlic / garlic purée
200g tinned black beans
5 cherry tomatoes
1 roasted red pepper (from a jar)
Half an avocado
Juice of half a lime
Handful fresh coriander
2 tortilla wraps

1. Heat the oil in a small frying pan. Peel and slice the onion, and add it to the pan, followed by the garlic, to soften for 2 minutes on a medium heat. Drain and rinse the black beans and tip them into the pan. Season well, and cook for a further 3-4 minutes, stirring occasionally.

2. Meanwhile, halve the cherry tomatoes and slice

the pepper into thin strips. Remove the stone from the avocado and cut it into 1cm chunks. Combine the tomato, pepper and avocado in a small bowl, and season with salt and black pepper. Squeeze over the lime juice and toss everything to combine.

3. Heat a second frying pan, and gently toast the tortillas on each side until just turning brown.

4. Roughly chop the coriander leaves and mix them into the tomato and avocado mixture.

5. Layer up the toasted tortillas with the beans and onions, then the tomato, pepper and avocado mixture, and serve immediately.

Sherry and Thyme Garlicky Mushrooms on Toast
Serves 2

Chestnut mushrooms are superb for this sort of dish, as they retain their bite and 'meaty' texture when cooked. But do mix them with other varieties for a proper fungi feast. Here, I've pulled out all the stops with a splash of sherry, garlic and fresh thyme.

1 tbsp rapeseed or sunflower oil
400g mushrooms (chestnut, flat cap or button,
  or a mixture)
1 tsp ready-chopped garlic / garlic purée
5 stalks fresh thyme
4 tbsp sherry ‑[CHECK]
2 large or 4 small slices sourdough bread ‑[CHECK]

1. Heat the oil in a large frying pan. Quarter the mushrooms, and add them to the pan with the garlic. Season generously, and cook over a fairly high heat for 4-5 minutes.

2. Strip the thyme leaves from their stalks and add them to the pan, discarding the stalks.

3. Pour in the sherry, and allow it to bubble for 1 minute, then remove the pan from the heat.

4. Toast the sourdough slices. Put a piece of toast on each plate and arrange the mushrooms on top.

SMALL PLATES

Cannellini Beans with Cavolo Nero
Serves 2

Cavolo nero (or black kale) is also known as 'dino kale' in the US, presumably because the leaves look uncannily like the skin of a reptile. It is dark green, packed with nutrients and has a deep, mineral-y sweetness and bobbly texture. Stir-frying it brings out the best of its flavour and texture, and it is perfect in this simple cherry tomato sauce with creamy cannellini beans.

You can serve this versatile dish in many different ways – with a crisp summer salad or with roasted winter veg, as a baked potato filling or even scooped up in flatbreads. If you can't find cavolo nero, then curly kale or finely sliced savoy cabbage make fine alternatives.

Olive oil for frying
1 red onion
1 tsp ready-chopped garlic / garlic purée
400g tin cannellini beans
400g tin cherry tomatoes
Pinch of sugar
100g cavolo nero (black kale)

1. Heat the oil in a frying pan. Peel and finely chop the red onion, and add it to the pan with the garlic. Cook for 2 minutes until it is starting to soften.

2. Drain and rinse the cannellini beans and add them to the frying pan, followed by the tin of cherry tomatoes in all their juice. Swill out the tomato tin with a little water (no more than a quarter full), and tip this into the pan, along with the sugar. Season with salt and pepper then stir and simmer on a medium heat.

3. Cut out the thick stalks from the centre of the cavolo nero leaves, then slice the leaves into rough bite-sized chunks. Heat a drizzle of oil in a second frying pan and stir-fry the cavolo nero for 3-4 minutes until crispy.

4. Mix the cavolo into the beans and tomato sauce. Taste and add more salt and black pepper if required, then serve.

Top Tip: Tinned cherry tomatoes are a little more expensive than standard chopped tomatoes, but worth every penny in a very simple sauce like this one. The juice they come in is thick and rich, which gives you a great head start.

Peanut Vietnamese Rolls
Serves 2 as a starter or snack

If you've ever tried a Vietnamese roll, you will probably be surprised to see them in a 15-minute recipe book, as they look like an awful fiddle to make. In fact they couldn't be easier.

50g pre-cooked fine rice noodles (from the chiller cabinet)
2 tsp soy sauce
Half a carrot
1 spring onion
Small handful fresh coriander leaves
2 tbsp chilli-coated peanuts
Small handful fresh beansprouts
4 spring roll wrappers
Sweet chilli dipping sauce

1. Cook the noodles according to the packet instructions. Tip them into a bowl, drizzle over the soy sauce and toss to mix it through the noodles.

2. To prepare the fillings, peel and then grate or julienne the carrot. Peel and finely slice the spring onion. Remove the coriander leaves and discard the stalks. Crush the peanuts in a pestle and mortar or chop them roughly.

3. Fill a large, shallow bowl or large frying pan with very warm water (not boiling – you will need to put your fingers in it). Place one of the spring roll

wrappers into the water and soak it for 10-15 seconds until soft, then lay it out flat on a large plate or chopping board.

4. Pile up the fillings in a line across the centre of the wrapper, starting with a few coriander leaves, peanuts, then a quarter of the noodles, spring onions, beansprouts and carrots. Fold in the two ends of the wrapper, then fold over one side to enclose the filling, and finally roll the whole thing up into a long tube shape, letting the wrapper stick to itself to completely seal in the fillings. Repeat with the remaining three spring roll wrappers.

5. Fill a small bowl with sweet chilli dipping sauce, and serve.

Curried Lentils with Spiced Cauliflower
Serves 2

A warmly spiced lentil dhal is one of my favourite vegan suppers, and this version is a speedy alternative. The spiced cauliflower keeps its crunch as it fries, while soaking up the fragrant cumin and turmeric.

I recently made some homemade stuffed naan breads using these spiced lentils as a filling, and they were absolutely delicious – give it a try!

For the spiced cauliflower:
2 tbsp rapeseed or sunflower oil
Half a cauliflower
1 tsp ground cumin
1 tsp ground turmeric
Small handful fresh coriander

For the spiced lentils:
1 tbsp rapeseed or sunflower oil
1 tsp ready-chopped garlic / garlic purée
1 tsp ready-chopped ginger / ginger purée
1 tsp ground cumin
1 tsp ground turmeric
1 green chilli
5 white mushrooms
400g tin green lentils
250ml water
Large handful baby spinach

1. Heat the oil in a large lidded frying pan. Remove the leaves from the cauliflower and cut it into small florets. Add the cumin and turmeric to the pan, followed by the cauliflower florets and mix everything well. Season with salt, then cover the pan with a lid and cook on a medium heat, stirring regularly, for 10 minutes or until the florets are just tender.

2. Meanwhile, to make the spiced lentils: heat the oil in a large lidded saucepan, and add the garlic, ginger, cumin and turmeric. De-seed and finely chop the chilli and stir it into the spices. Finely slice the mushrooms and put these in too.

3. Drain and rinse the lentils, then add them to the pan along with the water, seasoning well with salt,. Bring the lentils to the boil, cover and simmer for 5-6 minutes until tender.

4. Roughly chop the spinach and stir through the lentils. If they are looking dry, add 2 tbsp water and stir. Serve the lentils topped with the cauliflower and some roughly torn coriander leaves.

Pea Pâté with Pea Shoots on Sourdough Toast
Makes enough pâté for 6-8 slices

These gorgeously green, garlicky and lemony sourdough toasts make a simple starter or party snack. Many people don't realise that peas are a great source of protein.

This pâté does start to discolour slightly after about 10 minutes, so if you're planning to make it ahead of time, cover the bowl with cling film (pressing it down so it is touching the surface of the pâté), then spread it on toast right at the last minute.

300g frozen peas
2 tbsp olive or rapeseed oil
1 tsp ready-chopped garlic / garlic purée
1 lemon
Handful fresh mint leaves
2 tbsp cashew nuts
Sliced sourdough bread ─CHECK⟩
Handful pea shoots (rocket or watercress also work well)

1. Fill a small saucepan with boiling water, add the peas and boil for 3-4 minutes.

2. Meanwhile, heat the oil and garlic in a small frying pan over a gentle heat, until the garlic is just starting to sizzle (not turning brown). Cook for 2 minutes then remove from the heat to cool.

3. Drain the peas, rinse them well under cold water to

cool them down, then put them in a blender or food processor.

4. Add the garlic oil, the zest of the lemon and juice of half the lemon along with the mint leaves, cashews, and a generous seasoning of salt and black pepper. Blitz it all to a smooth purée (you may need to stop a couple of times to push the mint leaves right into the blades).

5. Toast the sourdough slices, and when they have cooled a little, spread them with the pea pâté, top with a few pea shoots and grind over a little more black pepper.

Courgetti and Sweetcorn Fritters with Coconut Yoghurt
Makes 6-8 small fritters

Chickpea flour is a vegan's friend, and is used in this recipe to make a delicious batter without the need for egg or milk. You can throw any combination of grated or finely chopped vegetables and herbs into these fritters – a great way of using up leftovers from the back of the fridge.

150g ready-made courgette spaghetti (or grated courgette)
75g chickpea (gram) flour
2 tsp curry powder (medium or hot, as you prefer)
½ tsp salt
3 spring onions
50g tinned sweetcorn
Rapeseed or sunflower oil for frying
100ml dairy-free coconut yoghurt
1 tbsp fresh mint
1 tbsp fresh coriander

1. Microwave the courgette spaghetti for 1½ minutes on high (either in its packet or in a small bowl covered with cling film). Tip it out onto a piece of kitchen paper to remove any excess moisture, and pat dry.

2. Tip the flour, curry powder and salt into a large bowl, and add water, mixing as you go, until a smooth batter has formed (roughly the consistency of cream).

3. Trim and finely slice the spring onions, and add them to the batter. If the courgetti is in very long strands, chop it roughly into shorter lengths. Add it to the batter followed by the sweetcorn. Mix it all together until everything is evenly coated.

4. Cover the bottom of a large frying pan with 2-3mm oil and heat to a medium-high heat. Drop in a table-spoon of the mixture, roughly shaping it into a circle, then repeat to cook 5 or 6 small fritters at once. Cook them until golden brown and crispy on both sides (roughly 2 minutes on each side), then remove the fritters from the pan, drain them on kitchen paper to remove excess oil, and continue until all the mixture has been used up.

5. Finally, chop the coriander and mint, and stir it through the coconut yoghurt, followed by a pinch of salt. Serve the fritters alongside a small bowl of the herby yoghurt.

Smoky 'Cowboy Beans'
Serves 2

When you've had a busy day at the ranch, these flavour-packed beans are just the comfort-food you need – smoky, sweet and slightly spicy. I like adding some sliced avocado on top and a squeeze of lime for some extra zing.

They are even better the next day, so I have included enough here for a bit extra: day-old cowboy beans (kept overnight in the fridge) are the best jacket potato filling I've come across.

2 tbsp rapeseed or sunflower oil
1 onion
1 carrot
1 red chilli
1 tsp ready-chopped garlic / garlic purée
1½ tsp ground cumin
1½ tsp smoked paprika
400g tin mixed beans
500g passata
2 tbsp brown sauce
1 tbsp dark brown sugar

1. Peel the onion and carrot and cut them into large chunks. De-seed the chilli and slice it into 4 or 5 pieces. Place all of these in a food processor, and blitz until finely chopped (but not a purée).

2. Heat the oil in a deep, lidded frying pan and tip in the blitzed vegetables. Stir in the garlic, cumin and smoked paprika. Cook on a high heat, stirring frequently, for 2 minutes, or until they start to soften.

3. Drain and rinse the beans then pour them into the pan, followed by the passata, brown sauce, sugar, and a generous seasoning of salt and pepper. Bring to the boil, then replace the lid and simmer on a medium-high heat for a good 8-10 minutes, stirring occasionally, until ready to serve.

Broad Beans and Asparagus with Lemon Breadcrumbs
Serves 2

This dish is full of the flavours of spring, though you can use the same basic formula to make use of whatever vegetables are in season.

Crispy garlic and lemon breadcrumbs do a very similar job to a grating of parmesan over a dish – they add a salty crunch and a pop of flavour, without any need for cheese.

1 slice bread CHECK
Olive oil for frying
1 tsp ready-chopped garlic / garlic purée
1 lemon
10 asparagus spears
6 tbsp frozen (or fresh, podded) broad beans
4 tbsp frozen (or fresh) peas
1 tbsp extra virgin olive oil

1. Toast the slice of bread, then blitz it into breadcrumbs in a food processor.

2. Heat the oil in a small frying pan and add the garlic. Let it sizzle for a minute, then tip in the breadcrumbs. Cook them until crisp and golden brown, stirring all the time, then remove from the heat. Zest the lemon directly onto the breadcrumbs with some salt and pepper and stir through. (Don't discard the

lemon, you will need the juice later).

3. Fill a large saucepan with boiling water and add a pinch of salt. Trim the woody ends from the asparagus spears and slice them diagonally into 3 or 4 pieces. Add the asparagus to the pan along with the broad beans and peas, and cook for 4 minutes until just tender.

3. In a mug or a small bowl, combine the extra virgin olive oil and juice of half the lemon, with a generous pinch of salt and ground black pepper. Whisk with a fork to make a dressing.

4. Drain the vegetables, then return them to the saucepan, pour over the dressing and toss to combine. Divide between the plates and scatter over the breadcrumbs before serving.

French Beans and New Potatoes with Fresh Basil Pesto
Serves 2

Peppery basil, lots of lemon juice and crunchy pine nuts are a wonderful coating for new potatoes and French beans. This is good hot as a side dish, or cold as a substantial salad to take on a picnic alongside some crisp green leaves.

If you haven't tried vegan parmesan, which is turning up in more and more supermarkets (or available online), I urge you to give it a go in a dish like this – a little grated over the top of these pesto-drenched vegetables really sets off their flavours.

150g baby new potatoes
100g fine green beans
15g fresh basil
½ tsp ready-chopped garlic / garlic purée
25g pine nuts
1½ tbsp extra virgin olive oil
Juice of half a lemon
1 tbsp vegan parmesan cheese or nutritional yeast flakes
  (optional) plus extra for finishing
1-2 tbsp water

1. Cut the potatoes into slices the thickness of a £1 coin, (there's no need to peel them), then add to a saucepan of salted boiling water. Bring to the boil, then set a timer for 4 minutes.

2. Trim the French beans, then add to the pan when the timer goes off, and cook for a further 4 minutes.

3. Make the pesto in a food processor or a pestle and mortar, by blitzing (or crushing) together the basil, garlic, pine nuts, olive oil, lemon juice, vegan parmesan or nutritional yeast flakes (if using), and a generous pinch of salt and black pepper to form a fairly smooth paste. You can add water a little at a time to loosen the consistency to that of a thick pouring sauce.

4. When the potatoes and beans are cooked through, drain them, return them to the saucepan and stir through the pesto. Serve scattered with a little grated vegan parmesan.

MAIN DISHES

One-Pot Linguine with Olives, Capers and Sun-Dried Tomatoes
Serves 2

When I first heard about one-pot pasta – cooking both the pasta and sauce in the same pot at the same time – I was dubious. Then I tried it and the results were incredible. The pasta was indeed cooked through properly and infused with all the flavours of the sauce, and the sauce itself was rich and glossy, thickened by the starch from the cooking pasta, and totally delicious.

200g dried linguine (or spaghetti)
500g passata with onion and garlic
1 red chilli
6 slices sun-dried tomato (from a jar)
50g pitted black olives
1 tbsp capers
1 tsp sugar
2 tbsp olive oil
Handful fresh basil

1. Find a large lidded saucepan in which the linguine will lie flat on the bottom, or snap the linguine in half to fit in a regular pan. Cover the linguine with the passata, then re-fill the passata carton or jar half way with water (250ml), and add this to the pan. Bring it to the boil and reduce to a simmer. Keep stirring whilst the pasta softens to ensure it doesn't

stick to the bottom of the pan.

2. De-seed and finely slice the chilli, drain and finely chop the sun-dried tomatoes, halve the olives and drain the capers, then add all these ingredients to the pan, along with the sugar and olive oil. Stir well, cover with the lid and cook on a medium heat for 10-11 minutes, (stirring regularly), until the pasta is cooked through.

3. Roughly chop the basil. When the pasta is cooked, stir in the basil and a grind of black pepper (it shouldn't need any salt), then serve.

Speedy Cauliflower and Chard Spelt Risotto
Serves 2

Spelt makes a delicious alternative to rice in this risotto; plus you can now buy handy pre-cooked pouches of it.

2 tbsp olive oil
1 onion
1 tsp ready-chopped garlic / garlic purée
1 stick celery
Half a cauliflower
75g swiss or rainbow chard
250g pouch ready-cooked spelt
125ml white wine (use water if you prefer not to
  use wine) ⬦CHECK⬦
175ml vegetable stock (with 1 tsp vegetable
  stock powder) ⬦CHECK⬦
Handful fresh parsley
1 tbsp dairy-free spread
2 tbsp vegan parmesan (optional)

1. Heat the oil in a large lidded casserole or deep frying pan. Peel and finely slice the onion, and add it to the pan with the garlic.

2. Trim the celery and cut it into a few large chunks. Trim the leaves from the cauliflower, and separate the central stalk from the small florets. Place the celery and cauliflower stalk (not the florets) into a mini-chopper or food processor and blitz into fine crumbs.

Add them to the pan. Cut the cauliflower florets into bite-sized pieces, and stir these in. Put the lid on the pan, and keep the heat fairly high.

3. Chop the stalks of the chard from the leaves, then slice the stalks finely and add them to the pan, replacing the lid. Finely slice the leaves, and set them aside.

4. Add the spelt to the pan, followed by the wine. Stir and allow it to bubble for a minute.

5. Add the stock to the pan, and season. Add the chard leaves and let everything simmer uncovered for 4-5 minutes until the cauliflower is just cooked through (it should still have some bite), and most of the liquid has cooked off.

6. Finely chop the parsley leaves, discarding the stalks. Just before serving, stir through the parsley, dairy-free spread and vegan parmesan.

Top Tip: If you can't get hold of ready-cooked spelt, brown rice or mixed grains would work well here too. Dried/uncooked spelt is available at most health food shops, so why not cook up a big batch then freeze it in 250g portions, ready to defrost and cook as above?

Creamy Chickpea and Kale Curry with Poppadoms
Serves 2

This is perfect comfort food with its warm spices and crunchy kale. Indian food is great for vegans as so much of it is naturally vegetarian and dairy-free. Serve this curry with mini poppadoms to turn a speedy supper into a proper feast.

2 tbsp rapeseed or sunflower oil
1 medium onion
2 tbsp korma spice paste (or medium curry powder)
400g tin chickpeas
1 red chilli
2 tomatoes
400ml tin coconut milk
Large handful curly kale
250g pouch pre-cooked basmati rice
½ packet mini poppadoms

1. Peel and slice the onion

2. Heat the oil in a large frying pan and add the chopped onion, followed by the spice paste. Sweat for 2 minutes, stirring regularly.

3. Drain and rinse the chickpeas, and tip them into the pan. De-seed and finely slice the chilli, dice the tomatoes and put these into the pot, juice, seeds and all. Season with salt, and stir everything together.

4. Pour the coconut milk into the pan, and cook for four minutes at a fairly high heat – the liquid should be bubbling vigorously, so stir it regularly to ensure it isn't sticking to the bottom.

5. Remove any woody stalks from the kale, chop it roughly, add it to the pan and cook for a further 4-6 minutes. Taste and adjust the seasoning if required.

6. Microwave the rice according to their packet instructions. Serve the curry with the rice and poppadoms.

Savoy and Sesame Flat Noodles with Marinated Tofu
Serves 2

For a long time I thought of cabbage in terms of stinky, boiled school dinners. Then I discovered crispy stir-fried savoy cabbage, and in particular the dream team of savoy, garlic, ginger and sesame, and have never looked back.

These flat, folded rice noodles are my favourite type, but if you can't get hold of them, any other egg-free noodle will do – fine vermicelli, wholewheat or soba.

150g Thai flat rice noodles (sometimes called folded rice
  noodles)
2 tbsp sesame seeds
1 red onion
2 tbsp rapeseed or sunflower oil
1 tsp ready-chopped garlic / garlic purée
2 tsp ready-chopped ginger / ginger purée
6 large leaves savoy cabbage
160g ready-cooked marinated tofu pieces (from the chiller
  cabinet)
1 tbsp soy sauce
1 tbsp sesame oil

1. Fill a large bowl or saucepan with boiling water, and add the noodles. Leave them to soak for 10-12 minutes until tender.

2. Heat a large, dry frying pan and toast the sesame seeds for 2 minutes until they start to pop, then tip them into a small bowl and set them aside.

3. Peel and slice the red onion. Add the oil to the frying pan, followed by the onion, ginger and garlic.

4. Remove the tough stalks from the cabbage leaves, then slice them as finely as you can (I find it easiest to roll them all together into a tube, then chop). Add them to the pan, followed by the tofu pieces. Cook for 4-5 minutes until the cabbage has softened a little and is just turning brown at the edges.

5. Drain the noodles and rinse under cold water, then add them to the pan. Use tongs or forks to combine all the ingredients and warm the noodles through. Add the soy sauce, sesame oil and sesame seeds, and mix until the noodles are coated. Taste, and add a little more soy sauce if required, then serve.

Spelt Spaghetti with Walnut Sauce and Purple Sprouting Broccoli
Serves 2

Pasta with walnut sauce is a dish from Liguria in north-west Italy. It is traditionally made with ricotta or mascarpone cheese; this vegan version gets its creaminess from dairy-free milk and the toasted walnuts themselves.

Don't skimp on the seasoning, particularly if you're not using the vegan 'parmesan' option – very simple sauces like this rely on every element being just right, so taste, adjust seasoning, then taste again!

250g spelt spaghetti (or brown rice spaghetti) –⟨CHECK⟩
200g purple sprouting broccoli
150g walnut pieces
1 slice bread –⟨CHECK⟩
200ml dairy-free milk (nut, oat or soya)
Handful fresh parsley
1 tsp ready-chopped garlic / garlic purée
2 tbsp vegan 'parmesan' or 1 tbsp nutritional yeast flakes
  (optional)

1. Fill a large saucepan with boiling water, add the spaghetti and a little salt. Bring to the boil and then simmer for 4 minutes.

2. Trim the woody ends from the purple sprouting broccoli, slice each stem into 2 or 3 (roughly 4cm

pieces) and add to the spaghetti. Boil for a further 6 minutes until the pasta is just cooked through, and the broccoli is tender.

3. Meanwhile, heat a small, dry frying pan and add the walnuts. Toast them until they are just turning brown and starting to release their oils (don't let them burn).

4. Tip the walnuts, bread, milk, parsley, garlic and vegan 'parmesan' (if using) into a food processor and blitz until fairly smooth but still a bit gritty. Season well with salt and black pepper.

5. Drain the spaghetti and broccoli, then return them to the saucepan and pour in the sauce. Stir well over a gentle heat to combine everything together. Taste and add a little more salt and pepper if required, then serve immediately.

Stir-Fried Tenderstem and Kale with Pesto Butter Bean Mash
Serves 2

The classic, velvety smooth *pommes purée* served in smart French restaurants sits halfway between mashed potato and a potato sauce. It's not one for vegans (or your arteries for that matter), with one part butter to two parts potato, but this butter bean mash instantly reminded me of that rich and luscious treat.

The great thing about butter bean mash is that it is packed with protein. Combine this with some crunchy, leafy superfoods and you have a knock-your-socks-off supper that's surprisingly good for you!

120g tenderstem broccoli (or purple sprouting broccoli)
2 tbsp rapeseed or sunflower oil
1 tsp ready-chopped garlic
75g curly kale
400g tin butter beans
75ml boiling water
½ tsp vegetable stock powder ─CHECK
1 tsp vegan pesto

1. Remove the woody ends from the tenderstem broccoli, and slice the stalks diagonally into 3-4 pieces. If any chunks are particularly thick, slice them in half lengthways.

2. Heat the oil in a large frying pan, and add the

tenderstem and garlic. Season well with salt and black pepper. Fry on a medium heat for 2-3 minutes.

3. Meanwhile, remove any woody stalks from the curly kale, and roughly chop the leaves. Toss these into the pan and cook for a further 3-4 minutes until both broccoli and kale are crisp and golden.

4. Drain and rinse the butter beans and put them in a food processor, followed by the boiling water, stock, and a pinch of salt. Blitz to a very smooth purée, then pour it into a small saucepan and heat it until piping hot. Taste and adjust seasoning if necessary.

5. Just before serving, stir the pesto through the butter bean mash, divide between two dishes and top with the tenderstem and kale.

Tahini and Cashew Quinoa Bowl with Garlic and Ginger Mushrooms
Serves 2

This recipe sounds like a bit of a 'trendy vegan' cliché, but it tastes so good I don't care! It's all about texture – nutty quinoa, crunchy toasted cashews, juicy mushrooms and crispy kale.

If you don't have any quinoa to hand, this is also delicious made with brown rice; similarly, a good substitute for tahini is peanut butter (or any other nut butter).

150g quinoa
100g cashew nuts
1 tbsp rapeseed or sunflower oil
1 tsp ready-chopped garlic / garlic purée
1 tsp ready-chopped ginger / ginger purée
200g button mushrooms
Large handful curly kale
2 tbsp tahini
Juice of 1 lemon
3-4 tbsp water

1. Fill a saucepan with boiling water. Rinse the quinoa thoroughly in a fine-meshed sieve under a running tap, then tip it into the saucepan. Boil for 12-14 minutes until tender, (and you can see the grain separate from the germ in little spirals).

2. Meanwhile, heat a large, dry frying pan and add the cashews. Toast them until they are just turning brown, put them in a bowl and set aside.

3. Return the pan to the heat and add the oil, ginger and garlic. Clean the mushrooms and tip them into the pan, and season well with salt and black pepper. Cook for 2-3 minutes.

4. Remove any woody stalks from the curly kale and chop it finely. Add it to the frying pan and cook everything for a further 3-4 minutes until crisp.

5. In a mug or small bowl, combine the tahini , lemon juice and water, and whisk with a fork until smooth. If it is still very thick, add more water until it reaches a pouring consistency. Season with a little salt and black pepper.

6. Drain the quinoa, rinse it under cold water and fluff it with a fork. Serve it topped with the mushroom and kale mixture, followed by the cashews and a drizzle of the tahini sauce.

Creamy Fusilli with Mushrooms and White Wine
Serves 2

A posh pasta dish that's just as good for a dinner party as for a weeknight supper. Dried porcini mushrooms and their soaking juices add an instant hit of deep, mushroomy flavour, and the juicy chestnut mushrooms and white wine make a lovely sauce with a slosh of dairy-free cream.

15g dried porcini mushrooms
200g dried fusilli pasta —CHECK
1 small onion or large shallot
1 tbsp rapeseed or sunflower oil
1 tsp ready-chopped garlic / garlic purée
125g chestnut mushrooms
4-5 stalks fresh thyme
125ml white wine —CHECK
125ml dairy-free cream (oat, soya or nut)

1. Put the porcini mushrooms in a mug or small bowl, and pour over boiling water until they are just covered. Set them aside to soak.

2. Fill a large saucepan with boiling water and a little salt, and add the pasta. Bring it to the boil and simmer for 10-11 minutes until cooked through.

3. Peel and finely chop the onion. Heat the oil in a large frying pan and fry the onion and garlic for 2 minutes until they start to soften.

4. Slice the chestnut mushrooms and add them to the frying pan. Season well, and cook for a further 2 minutes. Pick the leaves from the stems of the thyme, and sprinkle them over the mushrooms.

5. Pour the wine into the frying pan, turn up the heat to high and let it bubble vigorously for a minute. Drain the porcini juices straight into the frying pan through a sieve, then chop the porcini mushrooms finely and add them to the pan.

6. Finally, add the cream, and let the sauce bubble for a further minute or so until it has slightly thickened.

7. Drain the pasta and mix it through the sauce. Taste and adjust seasoning if required, then serve immediately.

Green Pea and New Potato Nutty Biryani
Serves 2

Biryani is a wonderful Indian dish in which rice, spices, potatoes and vegetables are cooked together in their own steam. The lid of the cooking pot is traditionally sealed with dough to ensure no steam escapes. This quick version requires a few cheat ingredients, including a pouch of pre-cooked pilau rice, but it really is packed with flavour and delicious.

1 onion
4 white mushrooms
2 tbsp rapeseed or sunflower oil
1 tsp ready-chopped garlic / garlic purée
3 tsp curry powder (medium or hot)
1 red chilli
5 baby new potatoes
150g frozen peas
125ml water
2 tbsp cashew nuts
2 tbsp whole almonds
250g pouch pre-cooked pilau rice
Handful fresh coriander

1. Peel and finely slice the onion, and roughly chop the mushrooms. Heat the oil in a large lidded casserole dish, and add the onion, garlic and curry powder, and then, after a minute, the mushrooms.

2. De-seed and finely slice the chilli and add it to the

pan, then slice the potatoes as thinly as you can and put these in, followed by the frozen peas and water. Bring to the boil, then reduce to a medium heat and cover with a lid. Cook for 6-7 minutes, stirring occasionally, until the potatoes are cooked.

3. Meanwhile, in a separate small frying pan, gently toast the cashews and almonds until they are just turning brown.

4. Cook the rice according to packet instructions. Roughly chop the coriander and the toasted nuts.

5. When the potatoes are cooked through, stir in the rice and coriander, and two thirds of the chopped nuts. Serve sprinkled with the remaining nuts.

Portobello Mushroom Stroganoff
Serves 2

Stroganoff conjures up images of a slightly naff 1970s dinner party, but there's a good reason why this classic dish remains so popular today.

I like to mix a few different types of mushroom together (portobello, chestnut and button), with their different shapes and textures. But use whichever you have in the fridge, or splash out on some wild mushrooms for a special occasion.

2 tbsp rapeseed or sunflower oil
1 onion
1 tsp ready-chopped garlic / garlic purée
500g mix of mushrooms
1 tsp paprika
80ml white wine ─CHECK⟩
1 tbsp tomato purée
50ml water
1 tsp vegetable stock powder ─CHECK⟩
100ml dairy-free single cream (oat, soya or nut)
Handful fresh parsley
250g pouch pre-cooked long grain or wild rice

1. Heat the oil in a large frying pan. Peel and slice the onion and add it to the pan, followed by the garlic.

2. Clean and slice the mushrooms into fairly large bite-sized pieces, and put these in the pan. Sprinkle

over the paprika, season well with salt and black pepper, and stir to combine. Cook for 4-5 minutes until the mushrooms are starting to soften and release their juices.

3. Add the white wine and bring the pan to the boil, then after a minute add the tomato purée, water and stock powder. Cook for 2-3 minutes, then add the cream and continue to cook until the sauce has reduced a little.

4. Meanwhile, cook the rice according to packet instructions, and finely chop the parsley.

5. Stir the parsley through the stroganoff, and serve it on a bed of rice.

Chapatti Wraps with Spiced Chickpeas, Baby Spinach and Coconut Yoghurt
Serves 2

These 'spiced' chickpeas aren't overly hot, just warm and aromatic. Choose a mild curry paste (korma is ideal) and add plenty of dairy-free yoghurt.

Use the biggest frying pan you have for the chickpeas – a larger surface area helps the liquid to evaporate quickly, leaving a more intense flavour (and less mess when eating your wraps!).

2 tbsp rapeseed or sunflower oil
1 tbsp curry spice paste (or 2 tsp curry powder)
1 tsp ready-chopped garlic / garlic purée
1 tsp ready-chopped ginger / ginger purée
Handful fresh coriander
400g tin chickpeas
400g tin chopped tomatoes
Pinch of sugar
½ tsp salt
2 chapattis
4 tbsp dairy-free yoghurt (coconut or soya)
Handful baby spinach

1. Heat the oil in a large frying pan. Add the spice paste, garlic and ginger.

2. Drain and rinse the chickpeas and add them to the pan. Finely chop the coriander stalks (setting aside the leaves for later), and add them to the pan.

144

3. Tip in the chopped tomatoes, sugar and salt, and stir to combine. Cook over a medium-high heat so that the liquid is bubbling constantly.

4. Heat another dry frying pan, and toast the chapattis for 30-40 seconds on each side.

5. To serve, scatter baby spinach leaves over each chapatti. Spoon over the chickpeas, and top each with dairy-free yoghurt and a scattering of coriander leaves. Fold over the edges of the chapatti and enjoy.

Top Tip: Don't throw away the water drained from the chickpea tin – this is the 'aquafaba' which makes an incredible vegan substitute for egg whites in meringues, macaroons, etc. Search the internet for 'aquafaba recipes' and prepare to be amazed!

Broad Bean, Fennel and Baby Carrot Pilaff
Serves 2

Full of the flavours of spring, this pilaff is quick and easy to throw together for an impressive supper. The fennel retains its crunch without being overpoweringly 'anniseedy', and really makes the dish.

2 tbsp rapeseed or sunflower oil
1 onion
2 tsp ready-chopped garlic / garlic purée (or less according to taste)
Half a fennel bulb
100g baby carrots
100g frozen or fresh broad beans (or a mix of frozen beans and peas)
200ml boiling water
1 tsp vegetable stock powder ─(CHECK⟩
250g pouch pre-cooked basmati rice
Juice of 1 lemon
40g walnuts
Handful fresh parsley

1. Heat the oil in a large lidded frying pan or casserole. Peel and finely slice the onion and add it to the pan, along with the garlic.

2. Trim the ends of the fennel, and remove the tough root from the centre, then slice it finely and add it to the pan. Trim the tops off the carrots, quarter them lengthways, and stir these in.

146

3. After 2 minutes, add the broad beans, boiling water and stock powder, then cover with a lid and simmer for 6 minutes.

4. Microwave the rice according to packet instructions, then stir it into the pan. Replace the lid and cook for a further 2 minutes on a slightly lower heat until the carrots are just cooked. Remove the mixture from the heat.

5. Roughly chop the walnuts and parsley, and stir them through, then squeeze over the lemon juice. Taste and adjust seasoning, then serve.

Peanut and Ginger Soba Noodles with Chestnut Mushrooms
Serves 2

Soba noodles are made from buckwheat flour and have a distinctive nutty flavour. They are often served in a clear broth, or chilled in salads, but I love them in this warm and satisfying dish. If you can't get hold of soba noodles, any other noodle variety works well, just adjust the cooking time.

For the noodles:
1 tbsp rapeseed or sunflower oil
250g chestnut mushrooms
4 spring onions
250g soba noodles (or egg-free wholewheat noodles)
2 tbsp dry roasted peanuts
Handful fresh coriander

For the peanut and ginger sauce:
1 lime
1 red chilli
2 tbsp sesame oil
2 tbsp peanut butter
2 tsp ready-chopped ginger / ginger purée
2 tbsp soy sauce
150ml water

1. Heat the oil in a frying pan. Clean and thickly slice the chestnut mushrooms and add them to the pan with a little salt.

2. Fill a saucepan with boiling water, and cook the soba noodles for 4-5 minutes until just soft, then drain and rinse them under cold water.

3. Trim and slice the spring onions, and when the mushrooms have been cooking for 4-5 minutes, add them to the frying pan. Cook for a further 2 minutes then remove from the heat.

4. Meanwhile, to make the sauce, remove the seeds from the chilli and roughly slice it. Squeeze the lime juice into a food processor along with all the remaining ingredients, and blitz until smooth.

5. Return the noodles to their saucepan, pour over the peanut sauce and heat gently until piping hot, (don't cook them for too long or they will dry out). Divide the noodles between two plates, and spoon over the mushrooms and spring onions. Roughly chop the peanuts and coriander, and sprinkle them on top, then serve immediately.

Sticky Black Bean Tofu with Cashew Fried Rice
Serves 2

If you haven't tried cooking with tofu before, this is a great way to start. For a long time I found it almost impossible to replicate that restaurant-style tofu at home, a super-crispy crust with soft insides, soaking up flavours like a sponge. But here are three easy tricks to keep it crispy and ever-so-tasty:

1) squeeze out as much liquid as possible
2) toss the tofu in cornflour before frying as a cheat's way of getting an extra-crisp crust
3) only add the tofu to the sauce at the very last minute and serve immediately, before it turns soggy.

200g extra-firm tofu (not silken – look in the chiller cabinet)
1 tbsp cornflour
Sunflower oil for frying
4 spring onions
3 tbsp cashew nuts
1 tsp ready-chopped garlic / garlic purée
1 tsp ready-chopped ginger / ginger purée
250g pouch ready-cooked long grain rice
2 tbsp soy sauce
120g sachet black bean sauce ⬡CHECK⬡

1. Drain out excess water from the tofu, then cut it into 1-2cm cubes. Place the cubes on a sheet of kitchen

roll, cover with another sheet and press down firmly to squeeze out as much water as possible.

2. Sprinkle the cornflour on to a plate and season with salt. Toss the tofu cubes in the cornflour until coated.

3. Heat a large frying pan over a high heat and pour in sunflower oil until the bottom is completely covered. When it is hot, tip in the tofu, and cook for a minute on each side until it is golden brown and very crispy. Use tongs to remove it to a plate, cover it in kitchen paper, and tip any remaining oil into a small bowl to throw away later. Set aside the pan, you will need it again in a minute.

4. Peel and slice the spring onions. Cook the rice according to packet instructions.

5. Heat 2 tbsp oil in a second frying pan and add the garlic, ginger, spring onions and cashews. Cook for 2 minutes then add the rice. Continue cooking over a medium heat for 2 more minutes then add the soy sauce and stir to combine. Divide the rice between two plates.

6. In the first frying pan, heat the black bean sauce until bubbling. Tip in the tofu and stir until it is fully coated, then spoon it at once over the rice.

Five-Spice Shiitake with Stir-fried Veg
Serves 2

Fresh shiitake mushrooms are such a treat. They retain their texture and 'bite' when cooked, so are quite the star of the show in a simple stir-fry like this one.

Chinese five-spice powder is an aromatic blend of flavours, usually star-anise, cinnamon, cloves, Sichuan pepper and fennel seeds, which adds a hint of the exotic.

2 tbsp rapeseed or sunflower oil
1 tsp ready-chopped garlic / garlic purée
1 tsp ready-chopped ginger / ginger purée
½ tsp Chinese five-spice powder
150g fresh shiitake mushrooms
1 head pak choi
3 spring onions
Handful fresh beansprouts
3 tbsp soy sauce
250g pouch ready-cooked long grain rice

1. Heat the oil in a large frying pan, then add the garlic, ginger and five-spice powder.

2. Cut the larger mushrooms in half, and leave the small ones whole, then add them to the pan. Cook for 2 minutes until starting to turn brown.

3. Cut off the root end of the pak choi, then slice the

white section finely. Add it to the pan with the mushrooms. Cook for a further 2-3 minutes.

4. Cook the rice according to packet instructions.

5. Finely slice the green leaves of the pak choi, and trim and slice the spring onions. Add both to the pan, followed by the beansprouts. Cook for a further minute, then add the soy sauce and stir everything to coat.

6. Remove the pan from the heat, and serve the rice topped with the stir-fried vegetables.

Quick Ratatouille with Lemony Chickpea Mash
Serves 2

Ratatouille is both delicious and versatile – leftovers make a great pasta sauce, jacket potato filling, or even a quick bruschetta starter on slices of toasted ciabatta.

There isn't time here to cook aubergine from raw (and under-cooked aubergine isn't nice), so if you can't get hold of these excellent frozen slices, just leave them out, and add a yellow pepper or a few sliced mushrooms instead.

For the ratatouille:
2 tbsp olive oil
1 red onion
1 tsp ready-chopped garlic / garlic purée
1 red pepper
1 courgette
5-6 slices frozen grilled aubergine
350g passata with basil (about two thirds of a 500ml
  carton or jar)
2 tbsp capers
1 tsp sugar

For the chickpea mash:
400g tin chickpeas
6 tbsp water
½ tsp vegetable stock powder ⫐CHECK⫐
1 lemon
1 tbsp olive oil

1. Heat the oil in a large and fairly deep frying pan or casserole. Slice the onion and add to the pan, along with the garlic.

2. Place the aubergine slices on a small plate, and microwave them for 30 seconds to defrost them slightly.

3. De-seed and slice the pepper and add it to the pan. Cut the courgette in half lengthways, then slice it thinly, before tipping it into the pan. Slice the aubergines into thin strips, and put these in. Season well, and cook for 2-3 minutes. Add the passata, capers and sugar to the pan, stir well and leave to cook at a fairly vigorous simmer until ready to serve.

4. Meanwhile, drain and rinse the chickpeas and put them in a mini-chopper, blender or food processor. Add the water, stock powder, lemon juice and olive oil, and season with salt and pepper. Blitz to a smooth purée, then tip it into a small saucepan and heat through until piping hot. Serve the mash topped with the ratatouille.

Top Tip: Chickpea mash is a great supper staple for vegans, as it is filling, tasty and packed with protein compared to its potato equivalent. It is great with veggie sausages and gravy, or as a topping for pies. It also freezes well so you can make a big batch when you have a moment and freeze it in individual portions.

DECADENT DESSERTS

Lemon and Poppyseed Waffles with Elderflower Summer Fruits
Makes 3-4 large waffles

Whether for a weekend breakfast or a crowd-pleasing dessert, waffles are a treat. A banana acts as an egg-replacer here (without adding an overpowering banana flavour) in an easy blitz-it-all-together batter.

You can replace the lemon and poppyseeds with all sorts of flavour combinations (orange and walnut, or vanilla), and for topping alternatives try peanut butter and sliced banana, or stewed apples with cinnamon.

For the waffles:
1 banana
150g self-raising flour
1 tsp baking powder
2 tbsp sunflower oil
200ml dairy-free milk (soya, nut or oat)
Zest of 1 lemon
2 tbsp caster sugar
Pinch salt
1 tbsp poppy seeds

For the elderflower summer fruits:
200g mixed summer fruits (fresh or frozen)
6 tbsp water
2 tbsp elderflower cordial
1 tsp caster sugar

1. Pre-heat the waffle maker according to manufacturer's instructions.

2. In a blender or food processor, blitz all the ingredients for the waffles (except the poppy seeds) into a smooth batter. Stir through the poppy seeds.

3. Meanwhile put the summer fruits into a small frying pan with the water, elderflower cordial and sugar. Simmer gently for 2-3 minutes until the fruit is soft and the sauce has become syrupy, then turn off the heat.

4. When the waffle maker is hot, pour in the first batch of batter, and cook it until golden brown. Repeat with the remaining waffles, and serve them topped with the summer fruit and a drizzle of syrup.

Top Tip: If you don't have a waffle maker, you can use this batter to make thick, American-style pancakes in a frying pan instead. Just cook for a couple of minutes on each side, and serve as above.

Gooey Chocolate and Pear Pudding
Serves 4

This is a pudding to serve to friends or family who just don't get the vegan thing – the ones who give you those pitying looks, the 'So, do you eat a lot of salad?' questions.

Gooey chocolate pudding studded with melting chocolate chips and lashed in chocolate sauce... need I say more?

For the pudding:
6 tbsp caster sugar
6 tbsp self-raising flour
2 tbsp cocoa powder
6 tbsp sunflower oil
6 tbsp dairy-free milk, (nut. oat or soya)
50g dark chocolate chips —CHECK
125g tin pear quarters

For the sauce:
100g dark/plain chocolate —CHECK
4 tbsp dairy-free cream (oat or soya)
1 tbsp dairy-free spread

1. Grease a microwave-safe ceramic dish or pudding basin with cooking spray or a little sunflower oil.

2. In a bowl, mix together all the pudding ingredients (except the chocolate chips and the pear), whisking with a fork until smooth. Fold in the chocolate chips.

3. Pour the pudding mixture into the greased dish, then drain the pear quarters, and arrange them artistically on top, pushing them down into the sponge mixture. Cover with cling film and pierce the top a few times.

4. Microwave the pudding on full power for 4 minutes, then test it in a few places with a knife – if it comes out clean, the pudding is ready. If not, continue to cook in 30-second blasts until it is cooked through.

5. To make the sauce, break the chocolate into small pieces in a microwave-safe jug, and add the cream and margarine. Microwave on full power for 1 minute, then whisk until smooth.

Top Tip: If you don't have a microwave, this will cook well in an oven pre-heated to 190°C / Gas Mark 5 for about 20 minutes, (no need to cover during cooking). The chocolate sauce can be cooked in a bowl over a saucepan of boiling water.

Banoffee 'Cheese cake' Pots
Serves 2

Before I get arrested by the sugar police, I should point out that this is most definitely a 'special occasion' dessert.

If you don't have a microwave, you can easily make the toffee sauce in a small saucepan; just keep an eye on it as it turns from liquid to solid in seconds.

For the toffee sauce:
4 tbsp light brown sugar
2 tbsp dairy-free cream (oat, soya or coconut)
1 tbsp dairy-free margarine
pinch salt

For the biscuit base:
6 sweet oaty biscuits (eg Hobnobs) CHECK
1 tbsp dairy-free spread

For the cheesecake layer:
100g dairy-free cream cheese
2 tbsp dairy-free yoghurt (soya or coconut)
1 tbsp light brown sugar

1. To make the sauce, place all the ingredients in a microwave-safe bowl or jug (with plenty of room for the sauce to bubble up quite a way without spilling over the top). Microwave on full power for 1 minute, then stir it and return to the microwave for a further

1 minute until it is bubbling and starting to thicken. Carefully pour the mixture into a cold jug or bowl (to help it cool down quickly), and set aside.

2. For the biscuit base, heat the spread in a small mug in the microwave for 30 seconds until melted. Place the biscuits in a sealable sandwich bag and bash into crumbs. Tip them into the mug with the spread and mix well.

3. To make the cheesecake layer, use an electric whisk (or a fork and some elbow grease) to combine all the ingredients in a bowl.

4. Take two glasses, and divide the biscuit base between them, pressing it down with a fork. Follow with the cheesecake mixture, and finally the cooled toffee sauce. Slice the banana diagonally, and place the slices on top. Chill until serving.

Amaretto-Sozzled Figs with Candied Walnut Crunch
Serves 4-6

Make the most of fig season with this deliciously simple topping for a scoop of vegan ice-cream.

It makes a really stunning centrepiece if you're entertaining, with guests able to help themselves to as much or as little as they like.

50g walnut pieces
75g icing sugar
3 tbsp water
2 tbsp dairy-free spread
Pinch of salt
4 fresh figs
4 tbsp amaretto (plus 1 tbsp for drizzling) ◁CHECK▷
Dairy-free ice cream to serve

1. Heat a small frying pan, and add the walnuts, icing sugar, water, dairy-free spread and a pinch of salt. Cook over a medium heat for 5 minutes, stirring frequently.

2. Place a square of greaseproof paper or baking parchment on a plate, and remove the walnuts on to the paper with a pair of forks, to cool, leaving any excess caramel in the bottom of the pan. Leave the pan off the heat for a minute, to cool.

3. Quarter the figs and arrange on a plate.

4. Return the pan to the heat, add the amaretto and bring it to the boil. When it has bubbled for a minute and thickened slightly with the leftover caramel, spoon it straight over the figs, followed by a final drizzle of neat amaretto for an extra kick. Roughly chop the candied walnuts and sprinkle them on top. Serve with a scoop of dairy-free ice cream per person.

Caramelised Peaches on French Toast
Serves 2

French Toast is basically bread soaked in an eggy custard. I've made an egg-free custard mix in which to soak a slightly stale fruit loaf. It isn't quite as crispy as the eggy version, but rich and custardy with a sweet, chewy crust – the perfect base for a fruity topping.

The peaches are at their best if cooked really quickly, so as to slightly caramelise on the outside but retain their firmness on the inside.

For the French toast:
1 tbsp custard powder –CHECK
2 tsp caster sugar
175ml nut milk
1 tbsp dairy-free margarine or coconut oil
2 slices fruit loaf or other sliced bread –CHECK

For the caramelised peaches:
2 fresh peaches
1 tbsp dairy-free spread or coconut oil
1 tbsp caster sugar

1. In a mug, mix the custard powder and sugar to a smooth paste with a little nut milk.

2. Heat the remaining milk in a small frying pan, and add the custard powder paste. When it has bubbled and thickened slightly, remove it from the heat.

3. Cut each slice of fruit loaf in half, and place all four halves into the custard, soaking them for 20-30 seconds on each side. Remove them to a clean plate.

4. Tip away any remaining custard, then rinse and dry the frying pan. Heat the margarine or coconut oil and when it is bubbling, add the slices of bread. Cook on high for 2 minutes on each side, or until crisping up and golden brown.

5. While the toast is cooking, halve the peaches, remove the stones and slice each half into 5-6 wedges.

6. Remove the French toast from the pan, and let the pan cool a little. To make the caramelised peaches, gently heat the dairy-free spread and sugar. When the sugar has dissolved, tip in the peaches, turn up the heat and cook them for 2 minutes until just turning golden brown at the edges.

7. Serve the French toast topped with the peaches, drizzled with a little of the peachy caramel sauce from the pan.

Top Tip: Make sure you are using the old-fashioned style custard powder, not 'instant custard' which contains milk powder. If in doubt, check the label!

Quick Raspberry Trifles
Makes 4 individual trifles

These trifles are easy to make, and look lovely layered up in tall glasses. You can serve them straight away, but they are better made in advance and chilled in the fridge for an hour.

For the sponge base:
4 tbsp sunflower oil
4 tbsp caster sugar
4 tbsp dairy-free milk
5 tbsp self-raising flour
½ tsp vanilla extract

For the trifle:
Ready-made soya or oat custard
3 tbsp dairy-free yoghurt (coconut or soya)
2 tbsp icing sugar
350g raspberries
2 tbsp flaked almonds

1. In a microwave-safe bowl (a cereal bowl is ideal), mix all the sponge ingredients with a fork until smooth.

2. Cover the bowl with cling film, and cook on full power for two minutes. Poke a clean knife into the centre of the sponge – if it comes out clean it is ready. If not, cook it in 30-second blasts until ready. When it is cool enough to handle, tip it out onto a plate

and use a knife to break it into crumbs to help cool it down.

3. Place about a third of the raspberries in a small bowl and mash them roughly with the back of a fork. Sprinkle with 1 tbsp icing sugar, then stir through 3 tbsp yoghurt.

4. Layer up the trifles: pack cake crumbs into the bottom of each glass, then spoon 2 tbsp custard over the top of each. Divide the yoghurt mixture between the glasses, followed by 2 tbsp custard per trifle, then finally arrange the remaining fresh raspberries on top, and sprinkle over the flaked almonds.

5. Chill until required, then finish with a dusting of icing sugar and serve.

Make it boozy: spoon 1-2 tsp sherry or madeira over the sponge base before adding the custard layer (just check your choice of tipple is vegan).

Chocolate and Peanut Butter 'Freakshake'
Makes 1 large shake or two small ones

There's only one rule of the Freakshake Club: don't ask how many calories they contain – that's just really not the point, at all. Even so, this is a relatively restrained version, topped with chocolate-drizzled popcorn in place of the traditional tower of whipped cream.

150g nut milk (hazelnut or almond work really well)
1 banana
1 heaped tbsp peanut butter
1 scoop dairy-free vanilla ice cream
1 tsp cocoa powder
1 tbsp maple syrup
100g plain/dark chocolate chips –⟨CHECK⟩
Handful sweet popcorn

1. Place the nut milk, banana, peanut butter, ice cream, cocoa powder, maple syrup and about a third of the chocolate chips into a blender or food processor, and blitz until smooth and creamy, (this may take up to a minute).

2. Set aside about a tablespoon of the remaining chocolate chips, and pour the rest into a small micro-wave-safe bowl. Microwave on full power for one minute until melted, and whisk with a fork until smooth.

3. Dip the rim of your glass into the melted chocolate,

then use a teaspoon to drizzle more of the chocolate around the rim to create the trademark Freakshake dribbles around the outside.

4. Pour in the milkshake, then top with as much popcorn as gravity will allow. Scatter over the chocolate chips, and then drizzle the whole lot with even more melted chocolate.

Oreo Knickerbocker Glory
Serves 2

No, I couldn't believe that Oreo cookies are vegan either, but they are – hooray!* To celebrate, here's a good old three-ingredient sundae, layered with smashed Oreo ice cream and crushed hazelnuts and topped with a whole cookie (it would be rude not to).

Vanilla dairy-free ice cream
7 Oreo cookies (or similar vegan chocolate cookies)
2 tbsp hazelnuts

1. Put 5 Oreos into a mini-chopper or food processor, and blitz into crumbs. Tip two-thirds into a large bowl, and the remaining third into a small bowl or mug. Put the hazelnuts in the mini-chopper and pulse a couple of times to roughly chop.

2. Add 4 large scoops of ice cream to the large bowl, and mash the Oreo crumbs into the ice cream with a fork. Put the mixture in a plastic container or small bowl and return to the freezer for 5 minutes to firm up.

3. To assemble, place a large scoop of ice cream into each glass. Top with Oreo crumbs and chopped hazelnuts, then add a second scoop of ice cream, more crumbs, hazelnuts and finally a whole Oreo stuck into the top. Serve immediately.

Top Tip: There is now a fantastic range of dairy-free ice creams on the market, and they vary in price quite considerably. There's no need to splash out on the really high-end or expensive ones for this recipe, as the star of the show is the crushed cookies rather than the ice cream. Cheap and cheerful will do nicely here!

*Please note that whilst Oreos do not contain any animal ingredients, their production lines are not separated so there is a risk of cross-contamination from some of their other products which contain milk. Whilst a lot of vegans are happy to eat foods made in factories with a risk of cross-contamination, some are not so please do research if you are concerned.

Chocolate, Chilli and Pistachio Dipped Strawberries
Makes 12-14 strawberries

There's something about dipping a fresh strawberry in chocolate that feels a little bit wrong, but you'll forgive yourself once you bite into one of these. Crisp, dark chocolate, crushed pistachios, and just a touch of chilli and salt add something quite wonderful here. Perfect for the end of a big meal, when you want to serve something sweet but not a huge pudding.

Instructing you to use a 'pinch' of chilli and salt is deliberately vague – be as tame or as daring as you like!

3 tbsp shelled pistachios
Pinch salt
Pinch dried chilli flakes
100g plain/dark chocolate CHECK
300g punnet strawberries

1. Crush the pistachios, salt and chilli flakes in a pestle and mortar (or chop them finely), then tip them on to a small plate. Lay a sheet of baking parchment or greaseproof paper over a chopping board or large plate.

2. Break the chocolate into small pieces, then microwave it for one minute. Give it a stir, then continue to microwave in 30-second blasts until it is just melted.

3. Holding on to the leaves, dip each strawberry in the melted chocolate, then roll it in the pistachio crumble. Lay it on the baking parchment to harden, and repeat until all the strawberries have been covered.

Quick Rhubarb and Custard Crumble Pots
Serves 2

This very simple layered dessert of stewed rhubarb, dairy-free custard and an oaty biscuit crumb topping couldn't be easier. The rhubarb here is fairly tart, with less sugar than you would use for a pie or crumble filling, as the sweet custard balances it out, but do add a little more sugar if you prefer.

The exact quantity of rhubarb and custard you will need varies according to the glasses you serve this in, but leftover rhubarb keeps for a few days in the fridge and is a wonderful topping for a bowl of granola.

3 medium stalks rhubarb (about 300g)
2 tbsp sugar
6 tbsp orange juice
4 sweet oaty biscuits (eg Hobnobs) — CHECK
1 tsp dairy-free spread
Ready-made soya or oat custard

1. Trim and finely slice the rhubarb. Place it in a saucepan with the sugar and orange juice and simmer for 6-8 minutes until soft. Pour it into a bowl and set aside to cool.

2. Place the biscuits in a sealable freezer bag and bash them with a heavy implement until crushed. Microwave the spread in a mug or small bowl until melted, then pour it into the bag and mix until

the crumbs are fully coated.

3. When the rhubarb has cooled sufficiently, layer up the glasses with rhubarb, custard, then more rhubarb and finally the biscuit crumbs. Chill until ready to serve.

Chocolate and Hazelnut Grilled Banana Splits
Serves 2

Bananas, cooked in the embers at the end of a barbecue, are one of my favourite fruity treats, and here's a 15-minute way to achieve a very similar result under the grill.

I've studded mine with dark chocolate and hazelnuts, but they are also fabulous with a splash of amaretto and scoop of dairy-free ice cream.

2 bananas
25g plain/dark chocolate CHECK
1 tbsp hazelnuts
2 tsp dairy-free cream (oat, soya or nut)

1. Turn your grill on to its highest heat. Cover a small baking tray with foil, and place the unpeeled bananas on it. Grill on one side until the skin has turned brown, then carefully flip over to the other side, and repeat (this should take about 4 minutes on each side).

2. When the skin is dark brown all over, make a slit in the skin from top to bottom, and open it up so the flesh is exposed. Return the bananas to the grill for 3-4 minutes.

3. Remove them from the grill, mash the flesh a little with a fork, then drizzle over the dairy-free

cream, sprinkle in the chocolate and follow with the hazelnuts. Return the bananas to the grill for a further minute or two until the chocolate is beginning to melt and the hazelnuts are turning golden brown.

Salted Caramel Chocolate Mousse Cups
Serves 2

This chocolate mousse is incredibly rich, so a small espresso-cup sized portion is just right. If you don't have espresso cups, any small ramekin or dish will do, just make sure it is sturdy enough to take the heat of the caramel.

I know the ingredients for the chocolate mousse sound a little alarming – silken tofu, really? Please just trust me on this one, I was as sceptical as you until I tried it, but this mousse really is magically airy and delicious.

For the salted caramel sauce:
4 tbsp light brown sugar
2 tbsp dairy-free cream (oat, soya or nut)
1 tbsp dairy-free margarine
½ tsp salt

For the chocolate mousse:
60g dark/plain chocolate plus a little extra for grating ⌐CHECK⌐
200g silken tofu
1½ tbsp maple syrup
1 tsp vanilla extract

1. Take a large microwaveable jug or bowl (with plenty of room for caramel to bubble up the sides without overflowing), and add the sugar, cream and margarine. Heat it in a microwave on full power for

1 minute 30 seconds, until it is bubbling and starting to thicken, then stir in the salt and pour the caramel into the base of two espresso cups or small ramekins.

2. Break the chocolate into individual squares and place it in a small microwaveable bowl. Cook it for 1 minute, then stir it and return it to the microwave for 30-second blasts until fully melted.

3. Place the tofu in a fine-meshed sieve and press out as much liquid as possible. Tip it into a blender, mini-chopper or food processor, followed by the melted chocolate, maple syrup and vanilla extract. Blitz until completely smooth.

4. Pour the chocolate mousse on top of the caramel, smooth the top with a knife, then grate over a little more chocolate. Keep the cups in the fridge until ready to serve.

Acknowledgements

Huge thanks to the brilliant team at Short Books for this opportunity to fulfil a long-held ambition of writing a cookbook, and to Sarah Williams at Sophie Hicks Agency for all she has done to make it happen. Also to Romas Foord and Henrietta Clancy for working their magic to create such beautiful photographs.

A fabulous team of recipe-testing volunteers embraced all things vegan, shopped for unfamiliar ingredients and cooked against the clock to give their honest and detailed feedback: my lovely Mum, Jennie Le Sueur, sister Sophie Le Sueur, fabulous friends Jess Dabbs and Elizabeth Beecher, Mary Dunford, Liz Dabbs, Andrew Le Sueur, Fiona Anderson, and Judith Parsons. Thank you all so much.

Grateful thanks to my family in Jersey and in-laws in Ely for their ongoing support, and the many thousands of miles they have travelled for babysitting shifts. And finally, to Andy: taster-in-chief, uncomplaining dish washer, sounding board, philosopher on food ethics, and critical best friend, whose many weeks of round-the-clock Daddy Daycare made this project possible (and who has probably eaten more vegan trifle attempts than any man on earth) – you are brilliant.

Author Biography

Kate Ford writes The Veg Space blog, which has been listed in the Top 10 Vegetarian and Vegan Food Blogs by the *Guardian*, *Red* and *Vegetarian Living*. Kate's recipes have appeared in *Observer Food Monthly*, *Vegan Food and Living* Magazine and others.

She won the 'Vegetarian Chef of the Future Competition' run by the Vegetarian Society and in 2011 was the creator of the 'UK's Tastiest Meat-Free Dish' for Linda McCartney Foods, which culminated in her Mushroom & Ale Pie being added to their range. Kate lives in Hertfordshire, UK with her husband and toddler.

Get in Touch

I love hearing from readers about recipes they have enjoyed (or haven't!), their vegan journeys so far, and their tips for delicious plant-based food.

Do get in touch, follow my blog for weekly vegan recipes, and tag me in photos of your meals:

Blog www.TheVegSpace.co.uk
Facebook www.facebook.com/thevegspace
Instagram @TheVegSpace (use #VeganIn15 if
   you're uploading your pictures)
Twitter @TheVegSpace

Index